HOW TO STOP BULLYING:

A KIDSCAPE TRAINING GUIDE

MICHELE ELLIOTT
JANE KILPATRICK

KIDSCAPE
152 BUCKINGHAM PALACE ROAD
LONDON SW1W 9TR

REGISTERED CHARITY: 326864

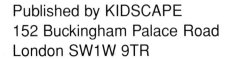

Published by KIDSCAPE
152 Buckingham Palace Road
London SW1W 9TR

First published in 1994

ISBN 1 872572 01 4

Printed and bound in Great Britain by
EJW Colour Print Ltd.
Swindon, Wiltshire

DEDICATION

We would like to dedicate this Guide to:

Dan Olweus, Professor of Psychology at the University of Bergen, Norway and the acknowledged world expert in the field of bullying. He has inspired and helped us all to understand the problem of bullying and how to stop it.

ACKNOWLEDGEMENTS

This Guide would not have been possible without the support of **The Paul Hamlyn Foundation**. We very much appreciate their generosity.

We are very grateful to **The Winston Churchill Memorial Trust**, which awarded a Fellowship to study bullying to Michele Elliott and to **Lt General Sir Richard Vickers**, former Director-General of The Winston Churchill Trust for his encouragement.

Four people have contributed brilliant ideas and exercises which you will note when going through the Guide:
Eric Jones, Deputy Headteacher and KIDSCAPE Associate Trainer
Pauline Collier, KIDSCAPE Associate Trainer
Enid MacNeill, KIDSCAPE Associate Trainer
Joan Preston, KIDSCAPE Associate Trainer

We gratefully acknowledge the hundreds of participants on the KIDSCAPE workshops over the past ten years who have not only experienced most of the exercises in this Guide, but have contributed many of the ideas which have subsequently been used in schools throughout the country.

For their ideas in sorting out how to deal with bullying, we are indebted to:
Linda Frost, Headteacher
Melanie Penders, KIDSCAPE Trustee
Anatol Pikas, Professor of Education, Sweden
Wendy Stainton Rogers, Professor Open University

To the **KIDSCAPE staff** who have worked with victims of bullying and their families and who have helped in putting together this Guide:

Gaby Shenton, Lisa Flowers, Angela Glaser, Daphne Joiner, Cath Bracher-Giles, Chris Turner, Helen Halliday, Liam Child

ABOUT THE AUTHORS

Michele Elliott is the Founder and Director of the Children's Charity KIDSCAPE. She is a Child Psychologist, teacher and mother of two sons. She has worked with children and families since 1968, is on the Advisory Councils of ChildLine and the NSPCC and has chaired Home Office and World Health Organisation Working Groups. She is the author of numerous books and articles on the subject of bullying and child abuse.

Jane Kilpatrick is the Assistant Director of KIDSCAPE and has worked with the charity for seven years. She has written several articles about bullying and child abuse. She also lectures and devises workshops.

CONTENTS

SECTION 2: WORKING WITH BULLIES AND VICTIMS –
CHANGING BEHAVIOUR   93

INTRODUCTION   93

RECOGNISING BULLYING BEHAVIOUR

WORKING WITH BULLIES AND VICTIMS

EXERCISES TO USE WITH BULLIES AND VICTIMS

SECTION 3: WORKING WITH STUDENTS –
LEARNING ABOUT AND DEALING WITH BULLYING

SECTION 4: RESOURCES –
BOOKLISTS AND ORGANISATIONS

INTRODUCTION: HOW TO USE THIS MANUAL

How to Stop Bullying: A KIDSCAPE Training Guide is a practical and positive Guide. You will be able to take exercises from it and use them with professionals, children and young people tomorrow, should you wish. Every exercise is based upon experience, common sense and good teaching techniques. The Guide is filled with practical remedies, theory and research. For those who wish to delve further into theory, see Section 4 which lists books about bullying.

Who is the Guide for?

This Guide is for all those working with children and young people in groups where bullying might occur. This includes:

Teachers, including those working in special schools
School pastoral staff
School nurses
Education Welfare Officers/Education Social Workers
Staff in residential settings
Prison officers in Young Offender Institutions
Youth workers
Health promotion staff
Police School and Community Liaison Officers

What is the Guide?

The Guide is divided into Four Sections:

SECTION 1: WORKING WITH ADULTS –
IDENTIFYING THE PROBLEM AND DEVISING A POLICY

SECTION 2: WORKING WITH BULLIES AND VICTIMS –
CHANGING BEHAVIOUR

SECTION 3: WORKING WITH STUDENTS –
LEARNING ABOUT AND DEALING WITH BULLYING

SECTION 4: RESOURCES –
BOOKLISTS AND ORGANISATIONS

Within these Sections are included:

Group Discussions
Course Notes
Handouts
Overheads
Roleplays
Exercises
Lesson Plans
Activities

The Guide can be used in whole or in part. Taken as a whole it provides an active learning course for those who have already begun to tackle the issue of bullying, as well as for those with little or no prior knowledge of bullying. Exercises, activities, roleplays or lessons plans can be extracted to be used as part of another course, or to address a particular issue such as racial bullying, or teaching assertiveness to victims of bullying. Though some of the exercises are placed in one section, many are designed so that they can be interchanged for use with professionals and students.

Trainers and others using the Guide can 'mix and match' the activities and exercises so that they meet the needs of individual groups.

The exercises for students and for victims and children who bully are, for the most part, adaptable for any age group. Hence we have not labelled them.

What should you expect to gain from the Guide?

Using the materials provided in the guide, you should:

● be able to devise an effective anti-bullying policy relevant to your own work

● be more confident in dealing with bullying incidents

● have developed and learned a variety of practical strategies and skills for helping victims and bullies

● be able to teach students through a variety of lessons about the problem of bullying and how to stop it

● be aware of resources and organisations which can help in dealing with bullying

We are continuing to revise and update materials about bullying at KIDSCAPE and we would be very interested to learn of your experiences and ideas. We would also be pleased to hear about any specific suggestions you have about this Guide. Please feel free to contact us at:

KIDSCAPE
152 Buckingham Palace Road*
London SW1W 9TR

(0171) 730 3300

KIDSCAPE is a nonprofit-making, registered Charity which teaches children about personal safety. With the help of parents, teachers, police and other concerned adults, children are taught practical ways of dealing with bullies, getting lost, approaches by strangers or by known adults who might try to abuse them.

KIDSCAPE provides full teaching programmes, books for parents and children, videos, free information booklets and posters. It also provides training in the use of its prevention and anti-bullying programmes. It holds frequent national conferences which raise new childcare issues and which pioneer effective ways of tackling the dangers which threaten children.

KIDSCAPE was founded in 1984 by Michele Elliott, a child psychologist, and the KIDSCAPE programmes are currently being used by over 2 million children and young people in the UK. KIDSCAPE raises most of its money by selling its teaching materials and training services. The Home Office has adopted the KIDSCAPE 'Keep Safe' Code in its nationwide Crack Crime Campaign.

* Offices sponsored by the Grosvenor Estate.

SECTION 1: WORKING WITH ADULTS – IDENTIFYING THE PROBLEM AND DEVISING A POLICY

1

INTRODUCTION

Working in schools and institutions with children and young people, it is inevitable that the issue of bullying will come up at some time. In order to make it easier to deal with, KIDSCAPE suggests that staff think about and decide upon a course of action before the problem reaches a crisis point.

This Section provides training for staff to help you set up your own anti-bullying policy and even gives you a prototype policy which you can use, adapt or discard (see later in this section KIDSCAPE: SPECIMEN ANTI-BULLYING POLICY). Although it is ideal if you can set up a training day, that is not always possible. The Section is designed so that you can pull out course notes and distribute them for staff to read and perhaps spend some time on one or two exercises, if necessary.

This Section has four purposes:

1) To help adults in contact with children and young people to understand why bullying happens and the issues involved

2) To help adults learn about the extent of bullying

3) To help adults set up a whole school/institution anti-bullying policy

4) To give trainers enough information and exercises to run training days about bullying

You may wish to incorporate some of the exercises and notes in Sections 2 and 3 which are also relevant to working with adults and to training days.

ONE-DAY COURSE OUTLINES

The following are two suggested outlines for one-day training courses on bullying with staff members. They have been used successfully with groups on KIDSCAPE courses.

1. The first course outline focuses on defining and uncovering bullying and on devising a whole-school/institution Anti-Bullying Policy.

2. The second course outline focuses on defining and working with bullies and victims.

KIDSCAPE: How to stop bullying

You may wish to devise your own course using the materials in this Guide – the various activities and materials could be used in a two- or three-day course, or could be condensed into half-a-day. Your circumstances will determine your use of the material.

COURSE OUTLINE: Defining Bullying and Devising an Anti-Bullying Policy

9:30	Introduction: Getting to know the group	page	6
	Definition of Bullying Exercises	page	24
10:15	Does Bullying Matter Exercise	page	15
10:30	Devising a Questionnaire	page	47
11:00	Contract Exercise	page	56
11:30	Break		
12:00	Suggestions which Work	page	77
1:00	Lunch		
2:00	A School Designed for Bullying	page	32
2:30	Producing an Anti-Bullying Policy	page	80
4:00	Discussion and Close		

COURSE OUTLINE: Bullies and Victims: Who are they and how can we help?

10:00	Getting to Know the Group	page	6
10:30	Recognising Victims	page	109
11:00	Assertiveness Exercises	page	144
11:30	Helping Victims – Exercise	page	127
12:00	Break		
12:30	Everyone is Valuable	page	230
1:00	Lunch		
2:00	Recognising Bullies	page	94
2:30	Changing the Bully's Behaviour - Exercise	page	138
3:00	A School Designed for Bullies	page	35
3:30	The Role of Adults in Bullying	page	40
4:00	Discussion and Close		

GETTING TO KNOW THE GROUP: *Exercise*

1

Object: For participants who do not work together to get to know each other

Time: 15-30 minutes

Choose one of the following exercises:

The participants sit so that they can all see each other. Ask each person to state their name and to explain why they were given their first name. You should limit participants to one minute each or you may find this exercise takes too long.

Although some people do not have a story about how they were named, many do. For example, one woman was called 'Carol' because she was born at Christmas, whilst a man called 'Aaron' had always felt aggrieved that his parents never looked any further in the book before choosing his name!

OR

The participants sit so that they can see each other.
In this exercise everyone introduces someone else.
Ask each participant to chose a partner and ask them to find out:

1. their partner's name
2. the name of their organisation
3. their role within the organisation
4. one interesting fact about themselves

For example, one woman said she had a cat with no tail; another admitted she was a chocoholic; whilst one man went pot-holing every weekend.

Allow two minutes each, and then ask participants to introduce their partner to the Group.

Both these exercises are fun and act as good ice-breakers if people do not know each other. It is also much easier to remember people's names if you know something personal about them.

TACKLING BULLYING – STAFF CONCERNS: *Exercise*

Object: To bring out concerns the staff may have about trying to deal with bullying and to give them an opportunity to discuss their worries

Time: 30 minutes

Materials: Copies of the concerns listed below

The staff of schools and other institutions quite often feel uncertain or even angry about having to get involved in doing something about bullying. It is another issue they are expected to deal with on top of all their other duties. Not unreasonably, there is sometimes resistance to becoming involved.

Divide the group into small groups of four to six. Give each person a copy of the statements listed below or make up your own. Alternately, you could have each group come up with their own statements, but this does take much longer. Each group should choose two or three concerns that they think are relevant and discuss them.

After about 15 minutes, ask the groups to come together and discuss their thoughts. You may ask each group to contribute only one idea so that they all get a chance to talk. You may also want to ask each group, or the large group, to come up with positive solutions so it doesn't turn into just a 'moan session'.

The following concerns have been raised in KIDSCAPE workshops – so you can see you're not alone!

Concerns:

1. Bullying is a normal part of growing up and I don't see what all the fuss is about. It helps kids to learn to stand up for themselves.

2. We don't have the time or expertise to deal with bullying. It should be done by specialists.

3. Nevermind the children bullying each other – what are we going to do about the children bullying the teachers?

4. What about the problem of bullies on the staff? There are some staff members who bully the kids and other members of staff. What can we do about that?

5. Most of the bullying takes place going to and from school. That isn't our problem.

6. I was bullied as a child and no one ever helped. Why shouldn't it be allowed to go on?

7. The real problem is that the kids who are bullies have bullies for parents. What happens when we try to stop their kids being bullies? Won't the parents attack us?

8. Won't it seem like we've got a real problem with bullying if we start to bring it out in the open? Will we get a reputation as a 'bully school'?

9. We already have a discipline policy. I don't see why we should have an anti-bullying policy as well.

10. This is just one more issue that is fashionable at the moment. I think we should just ignore it and get on with teaching – that's supposedly what we are here for. I've got more than enough to do already.

Believe it or not, there are still many people, including some teachers, who are not convinced that bullying is a problem or that it requires special measures. Perhaps this doesn't surprise you as these people might be the biggest bullies on your staff.

They argue that bullying has gone on for years and that nobody seems to be any the worse for it. Why devote a great deal of time and effort in an already overcrowded schedule to dealing with it?

This section looks at some of myths surrounding bullying and focuses on some of its immediate and longterm consequences.

Myths about Bullying:

"I was bullied at school and it didn't do me any harm"

This is often said quite aggressively as if the person is trying to convince him/herself that they are unaffected. The person may still be ashamed of the fact that they were unable to deal with the bullying themselves. They may never have faced up to what was done to them and how it affected them.

"Bullying is just a normal part of growing-up"

It doesn't have to be. To say to children or teenagers that they should suffer bullying and that it is OK and normal is totally unacceptable. Some victims remain victims for a long time or even become bullies and perpetuate the problem. If we feed the myth, telling them, overtly or by messages or acceptance, that bullying is normal then we fail children.

It is possible to create an environment in which bullying is not tolerated and in which aggression and violence are viewed as negative and wholly inappropriate types of behaviour.

"It's character-building"

Why does a child have to be tormented to the edge of despair in order to have their character 'built'? Character-destructive might be a more apt description. You can 'build' a child's character far more successfully by using positive role-models and by encouraging responsible, kind and helpful behaviour.

"It'll make a man of him"

This translates as 'You only become a man when you have suffered all sort of beatings/thefts/taunting in silence'. Why should a child be forced to suffer agonies in silence in order to become some sort of silent Clint Eastwood hero?

"There was bullying when I was at school but it didn't hurt anyone"

A comment actually made by a very hectoring and aggressive politician who had never recognized that he himself was a tremendous bully. He was oblivious to any suffering he might have caused people along the way.

"Sticks and stones can break your bones but names can never hurt you".

Anyone who believes this has never seen children reduced to despair by taunts like "fatty", "four-eyes", "taphead", "slag", "spaz", "Honky", "Paki".

"Only boys bully"

Boys may be more violent and more physical in their bullying than girls, but girls use ostracism (sending to Coventry), name-calling, and cruel comments which can be even more destructive to the victim in the longterm than physical assault.

"Don't tell or you're a grass"

This myth is one of the most persuasive. Bullying thrives in a climate of secrecy and fear. Unfortunately, for some children, telling has made the bullying worse. That is because the situation has been badly handled and the bully learns that not only are there no consequnces to his or her actions, but that bullying is more or less condoned.

Victims must be encouraged to tell and to see that telling works. Children and young people are frightened that telling will make it worse. But not telling strengthens the bully's hand and makes him or her feel that they can continue bullying. Telling makes the problem public. The bully's greatest shield is anonymity.

The school should ensure that bullying is dealt with immediately and effectively. The school anti-bullying policy should state that 'this is a telling school' and 'bullying of any kind is not tolerated'. There should be consequences to actions which are clearly stated and known throughout the school or organisation. The consequences do not necessarily have to be punitive – it may be that a meeting is set up or the bully is counselled and given alternative ways of behaving.

Sometimes, however, the consequences may have to be punitive, such as the bully being excluded from the playground for the safety of the other children, or in extreme cases, excluded from the school. But something must be done to stop the bullying or children will never tell again.

The Immediate Consequences of Bullying

When bullying occurs, there are usually immediate consequences for both the victim and the bully:

The victims may:

● lose confidence

● have their self-esteem diminished

● become withdrawn, nervous

● be unable to concentrate

● begin to do badly in their academic work

● truant, develop school phobia, attempt suicide

The bullies:

● and other children may learn that using aggression/violence is a successful strategy for getting what you want

● realise that they can 'get away with' violent and cruel behaviour and school discipline may be eroded

● become divisive as a dominant group coaleceses around bully – those not in the main group are left out and ignored

● become more disruptive – perhaps eventually testing members of staff to see how far they can push them

● suffer as their problems may be masked by aggressive behaviour and go untreated

1

LONGTERM CONSEQUENCES OF BULLYING

In additon to the possible immediate consequences of bullying, the longterm consequences for the victims and bullies include:

Victims

There have not been many longterm studies of victims of childhood bullying but at KIDSCAPE we have received numerous letters and telephone calls from adults who were bullied as children. They tell us that the emotional scars go very deep, and that the fear and loneliness they experienced as childhood victims still affect the way they look at the world.

Adult victims of childhood bullying can suffer from

- depression
- low self esteem
- fear of meeting strangers
- guilt, shame
- social isolation

- psychosomatic diseases
- agoraphobia
- anxiety/panic attacks
- exceptional timidity

They can also be more susceptible to approaches from cults and other unscrupulous organisations which play on their insecurities.

Stephen, now 24, wrote:

"I learnt not to get angry. I taught myself not to cry. It took several years. Even now I can't cry... I still feel very intense pain. The intensity of the feeling is quite difficult to describe - it altered my perspectives. For years I have felt dirty, degraded and ashamed... At times I feel intensely lonely. I get bouts of depression. I get anxiety attacks. Sometimes, for no apparent reason, I'll start shaking. These attacks are truly terrifying. I shake and have trouble breathing. Sometimes I hyperventilate. I feel I've lost so much time. So much of my life has been taken over."

Charles, in his fifties, wrote:

"The early attacks were because I looked funny to other young children. The later ones happened because I became withdrawn and 'seemed funny' because they were so awful to me that I did not want anything to do with them. Talk about a no win situation. If I read a story about child bullying, it sets off my bad memories and I am overwhelmed with anger, rage and tears, as though it was happening all over again, even 45 years later."

Robert, now 31, told us that he had moved to another town because he was still afraid of coming face to face with the people who had bullied him at school. He says that now he only feels comfortable at work where he is in a safe environment with familiar people.

Jane, in her late twenties, wrote:

"The bullying from girls in my secondary school was so intimidating that I went around for the whole of those years with my head down, trying desperately not to antagonise the bullies. I never could figure out why they hated me so much—I was so quiet and shy. I was so unhappy not having any friends that when a nice young man offered me a leaflet outside the Covent Garden Underground station inviting me to a free lecture about being more assertive, I screwed up my courage and went. Everyone was so friendly and welcoming that I felt wanted for the first time. They told me that I was intelligent and exactly the right kind of person to take their course.

The course cost £100 and, fool that I was, I gave them the money. The course was at their headquarters outside London. I went along and eventually got sucked deeper and deeper into what I now know was a cult. But at the time, I couldn't see what was happening. I ended up quitting my job, giving them all my money and staying in the cult for about 9 years. Looking back, I realise that it was my complete lack of confidence caused by the bullying which made me a perfect target for them. They bullied me into the cult. I am slowly getting my life back together, but it isn't easy. I think all young people should be warned that these cult people manipulate, lie and deceive to get their hands on you, they make you feel important and intelligent, but it is all a con."

Bullies:

Longterm consequences for adults who were bullies as children may include:

● uncontrollable and aggressive behaviour

● criminal convictions

● alcohol abuse

● child care problems

● employment problems

● unable to maintain longterm relationships – marital breakdown

● psychiatric disorders

In Professor Olweus's 1989 study* in Norway he found that children who were considered bullies at 12 were twice as likely as their peers to have criminal convictions and four times more likely to be multiple offenders. Typically convictions were for aggression and violence and were often alcohol-related. The longterm outlook for bullies is poor, especially for those children termed chronic bullies. (see SECTION 2: RECOGNISING VICTIMS - CHRONIC VICTIMS)

It is because bullying in children is so destructive, both in its immediate and its longterm effects, that we must take positive steps to eradicate it in our schools and institutions. It is not some inevitable natural phenomenon like thunderstorms or earthquakes which cannot be avoided – we can control bullying. If we want to provide a safe environment in which children can learn most effectively, its eradication must be a priority.

Olweus, D. 1989, 'Bully/victim problems among school children' in Rubin and Pepler, The Development and Treatment of Childhood Aggression.

DOES BULLYING MATTER?: *Three Exercises*

FIRST EXERCISE

Object: This Exercise looks at some of the myths surrounding bullying and focuses on its immediate and longterm consequences

Time: 10-15 minutes

Materials: Small cards

Is bullying a bad thing? Suddenly everyone is talking about it and doing something about it but, after all, bullying has gone on for years and are we any the worse for it? Do we need to devote a great deal of time and effort in an already overcrowded schedule to dealing with it?

Write some or all of the following statements on a flipchart. Ask the group what they think about them – do they agree/disagree?

OR

Write out each individual statement on a card. Ask participants to form small groups and hand each group one or two of the cards. Ask them to discuss the statements. Do they agree/disagree? After three minutes ask each group to feedback some of their comments.

"I was bullied at school and it didn't do me any harm "
"Bullying is just a part of growing-up"
"It's character-building"
"It'll make a man of him"
"There was bullying when I was at school but it didn't hurt anyone"
"Sticks and stones can break your bones but names can never hurt you"
"Only boys bully"

SECOND EXERCISE

Object: To focus on the immediate consequences of bullying

Time: 15-20 minutes

Ask participants to brainstorm the immediate effects of bullying for both bully and victim. Write down their ideas on a flipchart or board

Some of the *immediate* consequences of bullying include

* suffering of victim/s
* victim loses confidence, self-esteem diminishes
* victim becomes withdrawn, nervous, loses concentration
* victim may truant, develop school phobia, attempt suicide
* bully and other children learn that aggression/violence is a successful strategy for getting what you want
* can be divisive as dominant group coaleceses around bully
* bully's own problems may be masked by aggressive behaviour and go untreated

THIRD EXERCISE

Object: To focus on longterm effects and consequences of school bullying

Time: 15-20 minutes

Show OVERHEAD: WHAT HAPPENS TO BULLIES?/HANDOUT: WHAT HAPPENS TO VICTIMS?
This Overhead and Handout focus on the longterm consequences of bullying which may not be apparent to those tackling the problem with children and young people.

Show OVERHEAD: BULLYING AND YOUNG OFFENDERS and discuss the KIDSCAPE YOUNG OFFENDER SURVEY with the Group. Permitting bullying to flourish unchecked in schools has serious longterm consequences not just for the individual bullies and victims but for society as a whole.

Give participants time to discuss these ideas in small groups. Raise common concerns in the large group.

WHAT HAPPENS TO BULLIES?

1

The following adult problems have been linked to childhood bullying behaviour*:

* aggressive behaviour
* criminal convictions
* alcohol abuse
* abuse of children
* employment problems
* marital breakdowns
* psychiatric disorders

*Professor Dan Olweus in a 12 year follow-up study of 12 year-old bullies found that they were three times as likely to have a criminal conviction as the general population by age 24 (multiple offending was 4 times more frequent).

WHAT HAPPENS TO VICTIMS?

There have not been many longterm studies of victims of childhood bullying but at KIDSCAPE we have received numerous letters and telephone calls from adults who were bullied as children. They tell us that the emotional scars go very deep, and that the fear and loneliness they experienced as childhood victims still affect the way they look at the world.

Adult victims of childhood bullying can suffer from

- depression
- low self esteem
- fear of meeting strangers
- guilt, shame
- social isolation
- psychosomatic diseases
- agoraphobia
- anxiety/panic attacks
- exceptional timidity

Stephen, now 24, wrote: "I learnt not to get angry. I taught myself not to cry. It took several years. Even now I can't cry... I still feel very intense pain. The intensity of the feeling is quite difficult to describe – it altered my perspectives. For years I have felt dirty, degraded and ashamed.... At times I feel intensely lonely. I get bouts of depression. I get anxiety attacks. Sometimes, for no apparent reason, I'll start shaking. These attacks are truly terrifying. I shake and have trouble breathing. Sometimes I hyperventilate. I feel I've lost so much time. So much of my life has been taken over."

Charles, in his fifties, told us: "The early attacks were because I 'looked funny' to other young children. The later ones happened because I became withdrawn and 'seemed funny' because they were so awful to me that I did not want anything to do with them. Talk about a 'no win' situation. If I read a story about child bullying, it sets off my bad memories and I am overwhelmed with anger, rage and tears, as though it was happening all over again, even 45 years later.

Robert, now 31, told us that he had moved to another town because he was still afraid of coming face to face with the people who had bullied him at school. He says that now he only feels comfortable at work where he feels it is a safe environment with familiar people.

KIDSCAPE SURVEY OF YOUNG OFFENDERS, 1994:
Course Notes

KIDSCAPE carried out a survey of young offenders in March and April 1994 using a Questionnaire. The results show that unchecked school bullying can promote a climate of violence and aggression which encourages crime.

THE SURVEY

We questioned 79 young offenders in two institutions, HMYOI Onley and HMYOI Glen Parva, about their experiences of school bullying. They ranged in age from 16 to 21. We asked them whether bullying happened often in their school, whether they were involved in bullying, and what they thought schools should do to tackle bullying effectively.

We then personally interviewed 33 of these respondents. In the interviews we asked inmates to expand on some of the answers to the Questionnaire and we encouraged them to tell us about their involvement in school bullying. For ease of analysis and reference, we then categorized the inmates according to their answers as 'bullies', 'victims', and 'witnesses'.

We also asked the young offenders about their attitudes towards authority. 98% of the inmates thought that unchecked school bullying did make pupils less respectful of authority and 95% of those who admitted bullying at school said that getting away with bullying for so long had made them more likely to commit offences.

BULLYING: WHO IS INVOLVED?

The majority of the young offenders (62%) had themselves been bullies at school. 23% were involved as bystanders or witnesses who egged the bullies on, and 15% had been the victims of bullying. Of these victims, 07% subsequently became bullies; 05% committed crimes under the influence of bullies; 03% remained vctims.

When we asked those who had admitted bullying others at school why they had become bullies, the answers were similar: "to be number one in my year", "it made me feel big in front of my friends", "I did it to show off", "I wanted to show the girls who was best". These were typical responses. One inmate said that he was a 'nobody' at home but that at school he was "top dog and it was great".

Generally the bullies belonged to a gang. Only 6 inmates said they had bullied on their own and one of these was unusual in that he fought other bullies when their victims asked him for help. Two of the bullies said that they had joined their gang because if they didn't they would have become gang victims. However, the majority of bullies were either gang leaders or had joined a gang because their friends belonged. "I wanted to be with my mates" was a frequent reason. Gangs often had a 'hard image' and belonging conferred high group status on members. "It was really cool to belong to this tough gang".

Most of the victims said that they felt they had been bullied because of their small size or because they were quiet. The bullies admitted that they targeted weaknesses and what they perceived as differences. One victim said he had been picked on because of rumours that he was gay.

Only 8 of the bullies had begun bullying in primary school; the rest had started bullying at 12 or 13. Most of the victims had only been bullied in secondary school, although a few had been bullied for the whole of their school careers. Witnesses confirmed that, although bullying only happened occasionally in their primary schools, it was very common in their secondary schools.

WHAT SORT OF BULLYING?

The bullying ranged from name-calling and persecution through theft, kicking, punching and beating to assault with weapons. Threats were backed up by violence. Obtaining money or possessions like Walkmans or homework was often the motive for attack. Weapons involved in bullying incidents included a decorating tack gun modified to fire darts and wooden clubs.

OFFENCES

The inmates we questioned had usually been convicted of stealing cars (taking without consent or 'twocing') or burglary. It appeared that twocing was generally the first criminal act committed by most of the inmates and some then 'progressed' to burglary. Some also had convictions for GBH.

A couple of inmates said that they had been bullied into twocing – they were told that they would be beaten up if they did not go along with the gang. One victim said he had started to take drugs to boost his confidence and then had become a thief to pay for the habit. Some commented on the fact that the bullies had built up a 'hard image' for themselves and that, once they had all left school, they could no longer intimidate their peers so easily. Crime was one way of maintaining their 'hard image'.

KIDSCAPE: How to stop bullying

REPORTING BULLYING INCIDENTS

Two thirds of the victims said that they had never told anyone about the bullying. They gave several reasons for their silence: "I was too scared to tell", "If you tell, it'll come back on you", "I just tried to keep my head down", "I was afraid it would get worse if I told". The most common reason cited by both victims and witnesses was "I'm not a grass". Grassing was seen as a far more heinous offence than even the most violent of bullying attacks.

Although a third of the victims had told someone about the bullying, only one victim said that the adult he told had stopped the bullying. In all other cases, telling did not lead to effective action against the bullies.

WHAT CAN BE DONE TO STOP BULLYING?

All the bullies said that punishment didn't work and wasn't the answer to bullying, Perhaps this was only to be expected! However witnesses and victims thought that bullies should be punished as bullying is wrong. Almost all inmates thought that parents should be involved, and several thought that counselling bullies would be helpful.

If schools are to reduce bullying, we need to find ways of encouraging victims and bystanders to report bullying incidents. The taboo against grassing has to be broken. We should start teaching children to tell about bullying in primary school.

CONCLUSION

We found that 92% of the young offenders had engaged in bullying behaviour and had gone on to commit offences. 05% committed crimes under the influence of bullies. 03% of the total group of young offenders were and remain victims of bullying. The results of this one survey of an admittedly small number of young offenders indicate that there is a direct correlation between unchecked bullying behaviour and juvenile crime.

BULLYING AND YOUNG OFFENDERS

Kidscape Survey 1994

At HM Onley/Glen Parva Young Offenders Institutes

● **79 YOUNG OFFENDERS**

● **100% INVOLVED IN BULLYING:**

   ★ **62% Bullies**

   ★ **23% Witnesses**

   ★ **15% Victims:**

      ○ **07% subsequently became bullies**

      ○ **05% committed crimes under bully's influence**

      ○ **03% remained victims**

● **98%   thought bullying wrong**

● **95%   thought getting away with bullying made them more likely to commit offences**

DEFINITION OF BULLYING: *Course Notes*

Before drawing up an effective anti-bullying policy, it is useful to decide what is meant by bullying. Sometimes parents have said that their child is not *really* being bullied as it is *only* name-calling. However, any form of hurtful behaviour like name-calling can be classed as bullying if the bully persists with it after it is apparent that the victim is upset by what is being said.

A useful definition has been put forward by Professor Dan Olweus. He says that there are three main features present when bullying is happening:

1) Deliberate aggression

2) An asymmetric power relationship

3) The aggression results in pain and distress

Dan Olweus says that bullying is basically the repeated intimidation of a victim that is intentionally carried out by a more powerful person or group in order to cause physical and/or emotional hurt.

Although definitions of bullying may vary, this definition is widely accepted and could either be adopted as it is or used as a starting point to form your own definition of bullying.

TEASING

Sometimes people dismiss name-calling and verbal taunts as 'just teasing':

The word 'tease' is derived either from an old English word meaning 'to pull apart', or from a Norwegian word meaning 'to tear to bits'. To tease also means to 'torment or irritate'. Teasing can be cruel and destructive and it should not be dismissed automatically as trivial and unworthy of attention.

You will sometimes hear the excuse "We didn't really mean it. We were just teasing". However, students should understand that teasing as a form of bullying will not be tolerated. If the teasing is deliberate, repeated, aggressive and hurtful, then it is bullying. If it is good natured bantering between equals, then it is teasing.

1 DEFINITION OF BULLYING: *Two Exercises*

FIRST EXERCISE

Object: To enable group to discuss what constitutes bullying and to agree on an acceptable definition

Time: 10-15 minutes

This Exercise also indicates that what constitutes bullying can sometimes be disputed. It is important that schools decide what is and what is not acceptable and ensure that everyone in their school understands what is meant by bullying (this is discussed again later in this SECTION: WHY USE A QUESTIONNAIRE and SCHOOL CONTRACTS).

Ask participants to choose a partner. Each person tells their partner about one incident of bullying (either as victim or as bully) which they remember from their childhood. Give the pairs two minutes to exchange information.

Then ask the group if they consider the incident they have just heard about to be 'bullying' – very often, incidents perceived as bullying by one individual are dismissed by others as '*only teasing*' or '*just a joke*', or '*just part of growing up*', or '*too trivial to bother about*'.

Ask participants whether they think 'teasing' is bullying?

SECOND EXERCISE

Object: This Exercise helps participants draw up their own definition of bullying

Time: 15-20 minutes

Ask the group to think about their partner's story in Exercise 1 and any other incidents of bullying they are familiar with, and to come up with the key elements which make these incidents 'bullying'. You can note the elements on a flipchart/board/ OHP as the group calls them out.

Elements which groups have come up with on courses include:

power imbalance	humiliating	frightening
aggressive	persistent	belittling
secret	deliberate	hurtful
physical violence	mental abuse	verbal abuse
exclusion	ostracising	shaming

Show OVERHEAD/HANDOUT 'DEFINITION OF BULLYING'

This Definition is based on that used by Professor Dan Olweus of the University of Bergen, Norway, who has pioneered research into bullying in Norway.

Ask if the group agrees with the Definition or if they want to add anything to it.

1

DEFINITION OF BULLYING

THREE MAIN FEATURES

1. **deliberate aggression**

2. **unequal power relationship**

3. **results in pain & distress**

Repeated intimidation of a victim that is intentionally carried out by a more powerful person or group in order to cause physical and/or emotional hurt.

HOW WIDESPREAD IS BULLYING?: *Course Notes*

Whenever someone says that "We don't need an anti-bullying policy because there are no bullies in our school", we are suspicious or envious. Either they have actually set up a no bullying ethos without defining it, or work in a school with two students who are best friends, or they just don't want to know. One mother rang KIDSCAPE to say that her child had been bullied so badly that she tried to commit suicide. The response from that Headteacher was that the girl should 'pull herself together because life was tough all over'. On the other hand, we have very enlightened Headteachers and others doing their best to ensure that children and young people are free from the torment of bullying.

Recent studies have shown that bullying takes place in every type of school and occurs in all classes and cultures. It is much more widespread than was previously recognised. Bullying also occurs in institutions, the work place, religious organisations and agencies of every kind. It seems that little bullies grow up to be big bullies and pick on adult victims after they leave school. Of course, many of these bullies also make life impossible for their own children and families.

The first nationwide survey of bullying was carried out by KIDSCAPE between 1984-1986. 4,000 children aged 5 to 16 were interviewed from a random selection of 14 schools from South East London, Surrey, Newcastle, East Sussex, the Midlands and Devon. The children were asked about their main worries and concerns. Although they talked about everything from getting lost to being frightened by bad dreams, the majority (2,720 – 68%) complained of being bullied at some time. Most of the incidents occurred when travelling to or from school or in school. The bullying usually took place when no adult was present.

The children were then asked in more detail about their experiences: 1,520 (38%) of them had been bullied more than once or had experienced a particularly terrifying bullying incident. Of these 1520 victims: 1034 (68%) were boys and 486 (32%) were girls. 126 (12%) of the 1034 boys and 70 (14%) of the 486 girls seemed to be chronically and severely bullied to the point where it was affecting their everyday lives. These children who were so badly affected by bullying represented approximately 5% of the total 4000 children interviewed. Some of these children were terrified of going to school, often played truant, were ill, or had attempted suicide. It is this severely-bullied group which is the most worrying as their behaviour is self-destructive.
80% of the reported bullies were boys and 20% were girls. The vast majority of the bullies were at least one year older than their victims; many were 2 or more years older.* In more recent surveys carried out by KIDSCAPE, the number of girls reported as bullies has increased.

This is most likely because children and young people are beginning to realise that bullying includes being called names and other forms of verbal and emotional torment, as well as being physically attacked.

Other studies have been carried out in schools since KIDSCAPE's pioneering survey. The most recent was organised by the Department for Education-funded Sheffield Bullying Project which found that over a quarter of pupils (27%) in junior/middle schools in Sheffield were bullied at least once during termtime, and 10% said that they were bullied once a week. Figures for secondary schools were lower, although still far from negligible: 10% and 4% respectively.**

It is probably reasonable to conclude that at any one time about 1 in 7 children are involved in bullying either as victims or bullies. However, over a whole school career even more children will have been affected by bullying.***

The 1989 Report on Discipline in Schools chaired by Lord Elton found that "Bullying includes both physical and psychological intimidation. Recent studies of bullying in schools suggest that the problem is widespread and tends to be ignored by teachers..."

So, if you do an anonymous questionnaire (See this SECTION: WHY USE A QUESTIONNAIRE and DEVISING A QUESTIONNAIRE) in your school or institution and find bullying, don't be surprised!

---

* An Overhead of the KIDSCAPE results is given at the end of this Section for use in groupwork

** Whitney & Smith: A Survey of the nature & extent of bullying in junior/middle & secondary schools, in Press Educational Research, Vol 35, No 1 Spring 1993

*** Professor John Pearce in Bullying: A Practical Guide to Coping for Schools, ed. M. Elliott, 1991

KIDSCAPE BULLY SURVEY

- **4000   children, 5 to 16**

- **68%   bullied at least once**

- **38%   bullied more than once**

- **05%   severely bullied**

  - * **attempted suicide**
  - * **chronic runaways**
  - * **self-mutilate**
  - * **truant**

- **80%   reported bullies were boys**

- **30%   parents worried by bullying**

- **4%   parents tried intervention to stop bullying**

1 LESBIAN AND GAY BULLYING: *Course Notes and Exercise*

These Notes and Exercise were written and developed by Pauline Collier, KIDSCAPE Associate Trainer.

Developing a positive identity if you are a lesbian or gay in the midst of the ignorance, fear and hatred directed towards homosexuality is extremely difficult. Sadly, not only lesbians and gay students are affected. Those students with a lesbian or a gay parent can be bullied and isolated because of their family lifestyle. Matching up the negative, stereotyped images with a parent who is loved and respected can be a bewildering experience. Little effort has been made to understand and recognise the specific needs of young lesbians and gay men who often report that they have been bullied.

Much of our knowledge about lesbian and gay students comes from a survey carried out in 1984 by the London Lesbian and Gay Teenage Group Research Project. 416 individuals under the age of 21 completed a questionnaire about their lives as young people who identify themselves as lesbian, gay or bisexual. From their answers we know that:

* 1 in 2 had experienced PROBLEMS AT SCHOOL because they were lesbian or gay

* 1 in 5 had been BEATEN UP because they were lesbian or gay

* 6 in 10 had been VERBALLY ABUSED because they were lesbian or gay

* 1 in 5 had ATTEMPTED SUICIDE because they were lesbian or gay

Many schools refrain from discussing lesbian, gay or bisexual lifestyles for fear of contravening the much publicised Section 28 of the Local Government Act. This particular section says that local authorities should not "promote homosexuality". This piece of legislation, however, is only about what a local authority can and can not do and not about what individuals or schools can do. The Department of the Environment Circular says "...Section 28 does not affect the activities of school governors, nor of teachers. It will not prevent the objective discussion of homosexuality in the classroom, nor the counselling of pupils concerned about their sexuality. Such activities will continue to be governed by Section 46 of the Education (No 2) Act 1986..."

EXERCISE

Object: To raise awareness about the effects of homophobia (the fear and hatred of homosexuals) and homophobic bullying

Time: 40 minutes

Ask participants to consider the following statements on their own. They should decide whether they believe the statements are true or false.

After 5-10 minutes, ask participants to form groups of 3 or 4 and consider the statements together. Each group should try and reach a consensus.

After the group has fed back their conclusions, ask them to come up with suggestions which will help them deal with any cases of students being bullied because they are gay or lesbian.

Statements:

All lesbians want to be men.

Lesbians cannot have children.

One in ten students in your school/institution is lesbian or gay.

Gay men are a danger to adolescent boys.

Young people become gay because it's fashionable.

Lesbians and gay men should have the same rights as everyone else.

Children in school should be given information about homosexuality.

Gay men are born that way.

People are prejudiced against lesbians because they don't know enough about them.

Lesbians and gay men should be allowed to foster or adopt children.

Lesbian and gay men should not be allowed to become teachers.

You could also use this Exercise with older students.

Bullying Thrives: *Exercise*

Object: This Exercise is a 'kick start' to get workshop participants to focus
quickly on 5 reasons why bullying thrives and 5 ways to stop it

Time: 10 minutes

Materials: Paper and pens

This Exercise is not meant to be in-depth, but it can be expanded
should you wish. You can also use this with children and young people.

In small groups, ask the participants to come up with 5 reasons why
they think bullying can thrive in an institution, followed by 5 ways to stop
it. Tell them that this must be done quickly and they need to agree. You
can specify that the ideas should not be about buildings or resources
(such as 'we need to move the toilets closer to the school' – cost
£100,000), but ideas which are based on working with people.

It is a good exercise for energising a group and getting them to work
together.

Below is an example from a group on one of the KIDSCAPE
workshops. It can be used as a Handout or Overhead after the groups
have come up with their own ideas.

1

BULLYING THRIVES WHEN:

1. ADULTS SAY NOTHING CAN BE DONE

2. IT IS CONSIDERED 'A NORMAL OR ESSENTIAL PART OF GROWING UP'

3. CHILDREN HAVE TOO MUCH POWER OVER OTHER CHILDREN

4. THERE IS NO PRIVATE WAY FOR VICTIMS TO GET HELP AND TELLING IS DISCOURAGED

5. THERE IS NO ANTI- BULLYING POLICY IN THE SCHOOL OR INSTITUTION

1

BULLYING CAN BE STOPPED BY

1. CONDUCTING AN ANONYMOUS SURVEY

2. WORKING WITH CHILDREN/ YOUNG PEOPLE TO SET UP ANTI-BULLYING POLICY

3. ENSURING THAT THERE IS ACCESS TO HELP – PRIVATELY

4. TALKING ABOUT BULLYING – USING DRAMA, ART, ENGLISH

5. USING 'BULLY COURTS', TRAINING ALL STAFF TO RECOGNISE SIGNS AND SYMPTOMS

A SCHOOL DESIGNED FOR BULLIES?: *Course Notes*

Old buildings with poky rooms and long, dark corridors can provide a physical environment which promotes bullying. There are plenty of places where bullies can corner their victims, especially if supervision is inadequate. Outside buildings like bike-sheds can also provide perfect cover for bullying activities.

Even though we cannot completely rebuild our old school buildings, we can ensure that supervision is adequate and we can encourage victims to tell where and when they were bullied in order to pin down likely trouble spots or times. The Survey Questionnaire will also help to identify where and when bullying is most likely to take place.

In one school bullying was rife at break-times so the Headteacher moved his office to a room which overlooked the playground. Bullying diminished rapidly once the bullies realised that their every move could be monitored by the Headteacher glancing out of the window. In another school the problem was solved when governors approved the use of a camera which was trained on the playground during breaks. Just knowing that they might be captured on film stopped the bullying behaviour almost overnight and certainly eliminated the 'I didn't do it, Miss' excuse.

An awareness of the site of the problem and a flexible approach to solutions can often make the difference between promoting bullying and preventing it.

Adequate supervision of students is very important and playground supervisors and catering staff should be involved in the implementation of the anti-bullying policy from the beginning. They are well-placed to see if bullying continues to take place and to identify both bullies and victims.

Staff attitudes, the physical lay-out of the school and the adequacy or otherwise of supervision arrangements all have to be considered when devising a whole-school anti-bullying policy.
Other factors which can promote bullying are :

* low staff morale
* high teacher turnover
* unclear standards of behaviour
* inconsistent methods of discipline
* poor organisation
* lack of awareness of children as individuals
* staff remote and unapproachable

The HANDOUT: THE PERFECT ENVIRONMENT FOR BULLYING which follows the next Exercise identifies some of the things we should look out for when we decide to tackle bullying.

A SCHOOL DESIGNED FOR BULLIES?: *Exercise*

Object: To illustrate how physical surroundings and inadequate supervision, as much as lack of effective policies, can permit bullying to flourish

Time: 15 to 30 minutes

Materials: Paper and pens

Ask participants to divide into four groups and ask each group to come up with suggestions for a perfect school for bullies. Ask one person to write down the group's ideas. After 10 minutes, ask each group to feedback their ideas – you can write them on a flipchart or board. Groups usually come up with ideas which can be grouped under the headings below:

* low staff morale
* high teacher turnover
* unclear standards of behaviour
* inconsistent methods of discipline
* poor organisation
* inadequate supervision
* lack of awareness of children as individuals

After the participants have completed the exercise, you can give them the HANDOUT: THE PERFECT ENVIRONMENT FOR BULLYING and see if they wish to add anything to their own lists.

If participants apply this Exercise to their own institutions, it will help to focus their attention on the most likely places for bullying. (The Questionnaire should contain questions on location, asking respondents to say where they were bullied and where they thought most bullying took place.)

See also: SECTION 3: SEMPER BELLICOSISSIMUS – 2 EXERCISES FOR STUDENTS.

THE PERFECT ENVIRONMENT FOR BULLYING

Peter Stephenson and David Smith produced a list of what was needed to ensure a perfect environment for bullying.* The following list has been devised by participants in the KIDSCAPE workshops and includes some of the points made by Stephenson and Smith. The list is not meant to be exhaustive – everyone will have something to add! One participant said the list *perfectly described* his school.

unsupervised toilets
no space for 'quiet' activities
bare, empty playground
not enough equipment in gyms and labs
unsupervised playground
areas where staff never go
old buildings with dark, secluded corners
staff never around – always in staff room
staff too busy to notice incidents
staff too busy to do anything practical about reported incidents
unsupervised meal queues
whole school queuing at once for meals
narrow, dark corridors
crowded locker rooms
everyone arriving and leaving at once
long change-overs between classes
teachers being late
chaotic classrooms
staff leaving classrooms during lessons
no pastoral staff
bike sheds
teachers who point/shout/poke
teachers who use sarcasm as a destructive weapon
no support for pupils with special needs
unsupervised living accommodation
intolerance of differences
allowing hurtful graffiti to remain
headteacher and/or staff who bully
reporting bullying seen as 'telling tales'
'initiation' ceremonies for new students
no support for new pupils
staff who humiliate pupils in front of others
no anti-bullying policy
no clear procedures for reporting and dealing with bullying incidents
general lack of supervision and discipline
staff hoping issue will go away if it is ignored for long enough

* Stephenson, P. and Smith, D. 'Why Some Schools Don't Have Bullies' in Elliott, M. (ed) Bullying, A Practical Guide to Coping for Schools, Longman 1991 (available from KIDSCAPE)

ADULTS: WHAT IS OUR ROLE?: *Course Notes*

Adults affect bullying in three ways: they can permit it by their lack of concern for victims and by not tackling incidents; they can promote it by their attitudes and by allowing bullies to get away with it; and they can prevent it by taking action and by challenging bullying whenever it takes place.*

Bullying is permitted when victims are ignored or blamed; when adults do not listen to what children tell them; when victims who tell are told to sort it out themselves; when victims are too scared to tell; when adults encourage retaliation; and when there are no policies or procedures for dealing with bullying incidents.

Bullying is promoted when adults are dismissive of what children tell them; when adults are aggressive and sarcastic; when they humiliate children in front of their peers; when they pick on particular individuals; when they are impatient with the less able; when they are unapproachable and insensitive; when they do not set limits; and when classroom management is poor.

Bullying is prevented when adults listen to children and encourage them to tell about bullying; when adults are fair; when differences between individuals are celebrated; when adults raise children's self-esteem; when adults are assertive not aggressive; when policies and procedures to eradicate bullying are devised and implemented; and if adults act immediately they hear about bullying, fighting or cruelty.

If we are serious about wanting to tackle bullying in our schools, we have to examine our own attitudes first. If staff continue to display bullying behaviour, no matter how good the school's anti-bullying policy, students will get the message that bullying is acceptable. It is up to the whole staff to provide an environment in which it is clear that bullying behaviour is not acceptable in either staff or students. Children learn by example and staff should provide behaviour role-models for their students.

Professor Dan Olweus, of the University of Bergen and a leading expert on the prevention of bullying, concludes in his latest book* "The attitudes, routines, and behaviours of the school personnel, particularly those of the teachers, are *decisive factors* in preventing and controlling bullying activities, as well as in redirecting such behaviours in to more socially acceptable channels." (our italics).

* See: 'Promoting, Permitting and Preventing Bullying' by Wendy Stainton-Rogers in 'Bullying: A Practical Guide', ed. Michele Elliott, Longman 1991 (available from KIDSCAPE)

One way that adults can be decisive is to try, if circumstances permit, to mediate. In some cases an interview might be set up in which the bully is spoken to, in the presence of an adult chosen by the victim. The victim tells the bully what s/he has suffered, how s/he felt and how this bullying is affecting him/her. The adult listens and acts as a recorder rather than a judge. The bully may or may not apologise, but must at least listen and agree to keep what is said confidential. It may be part of the process of teaching the bully to empathise with others. However, this process of not judging or blaming seems to work best if the bully and victim have a previous good relationship or if the bully does not have a long history of troubled behaviour (see: later in this SECTION: COMMON CONCERN APPROACH). Otherwise the bully can use the information gleaned in the session to torment the victim further. Usually the teacher or staff member has enough knowledge of the circumstances to decide (with the victim) whether this approach is worth trying.

In other cases, the most decisive and effective way of dealing with the bullying is to tell the bully off, withdraw privileges, or impose other consequences. Possible consequences might include making the bully apologise, even if the apology is grudging; or assigning the bully to a particular place to eat or play or study until the situation is resolved; or keeping the bully behind at the end of the day to allow the other children or young people time to get home without fear of intimidation.

All adults who work with children or young people should try to perfect (and even rehearse) good, solid, straightforward instructions and requests - in the classroom, in institutions, on group journeys - anywhere that adults are in the position of protecting, instructing or ushering children around. These instructions and requests should avoid, at all costs, using bullying tactics and methods of control. Adults should try not to resort to shouting, to being abusive, sarcastic or insulting or to using belittling adjectives. By providing positive models of behaviour, adults can create a healthy atmosphere for the children in their care.

* Bullying at School: What we know and what we can do. Blackwell, 1993

ADULTS: WHAT IS OUR ROLE?: *Two Exercises*

FIRST EXERCISE – PERMIT, PROMOTE OR PREVENT?

Object: To encourage participants to focus on the role they themselves can play in preventing bullying in their institution

Time: 20 minutes

Materials: Paper, coloured pens

Ask participants to divide into three groups and ask one person from each group to write down their group's ideas.

Each group is asked to look at bullying from a different perspective:

Group 1 looks at the problem from the perspective of Children/Young People

Group 2 looks at the problem from the perspective of Parents

Group 3 looks at the problem from the perspective of Teachers/Staff

Ask the three groups to consider how they, as children, parents, or staff, permit, promote or prevent bullying. Ask them to classify their ideas under one of these three headings.

On a flipchart or board draw three columns and label them: Permit, Promote, Prevent.

After 10 minutes ask the person writing down the group's ideas to call them out. Write each group's ideas in a different colour on the flipchart/ board.

This Exercise can also be used at a Parents' Meeting to focus attention on the role parents play in encouraging and/or preventing bullying.

Points raised during KIDSCAPE courses include:

Permit	Promote	Prevent
Ignore victim	Dismissive	Raise self-esteem
Inadequate supervision	Poor classroom management	Listening
		Fairness
Dismissive	Sarcasm	Celebrate differences
Not listening	No discipline	Promote social skills
	Undervalue less-able child	Preventative strategies
Encourage retaliation	Aggressive role-model	Tell the school
	No limits	Boost confidence
	Not listening	Assertive
Lack of time	Unapproachable	
Lack of policy	Insensitive	Listening
No procedures		Anti-Bully Policy
		Procedures
		Immediate action

Some ideas will be produced by all three groups.

Adults permit and promote bullying by their own attitudes as much as by lack of clear policies and procedures to deal with bullying incidents.

SECOND EXERCISE – THE BALL OF STRING

Object: This is a simple and fun exercise which shows what happens if a school or institution does not have an effective anti-bullying policy

Time: 10 minutes

Materials: Overhead, ball of string

SHOW OVERHEAD: ROLES

Choose one participant as the 'victim'. Everyone else chooses a 'role' from the list on the OVERHEAD (this list can be expanded to reflect members of staff/community relevant to individual institutions); or the Trainer can allocate roles to participants; or participants can adopt another role of their choice. Every participant should have a 'role'. If anyone is left after all the roles have been taken, ask the group to think of ways in which this person could be helpful to the victim.

The 'victim' is given a ball of string which represents 'bullying'. The 'victim' **holds** one end of the string and throws the ball to a participant playing a suitable 'role' (mother, for example). This represents telling about the bullying and asking for help. Each participant keeps hold of the string which represents keeping hold of the problem and remaining involved in its solution.

The second participant, **holding** onto the string, then throws the ball to another participant playing a suitable 'role', and so on until everyone has caught the ball and thrown it on. At the end, the room should look like a cat's cradle with every participant linked by the string.

(For example, 'victim' throws to 'mother' who throws to 'father' who throws to 'teacher' who throws to 'head of year' who throws to 'head teacher' etc.)

The cat's cradle is a tangled muddle and it represents what can happen when there is no agreed procedure for dealing with bullying. Everyone gets dragged into the problem.

Now Repeat the Exercise but this time the bullying is occuring in an institution with an effective anti-bullying policy so you only need a few people because everyone now knows exactly what part they play in resolving bullying incidents.

(For example, as the instituiton has a clear policy, the string can be thrown from Teacher to Head of Year to Headteacher. Occasionally the string, representing the problem, might then be thrown to an outside specialist like an educational psychologist, but rarely does it have to go further.)

At the end of the second string throwing exercise you have a short and neat line of people with no tangles – everyone knows how they fit into the anti-bullying procedure.

OVERHEAD:

ROLES

BULLY
VICTIM
FRIEND
CLASS TEACHER
YEAR HEAD
HEADTEACHER
MOTHER
FATHER
OTHER RELATIVE (AUNT,UNCLE)
PARENT GOVERNOR
CHAIR OF GOVERNORS
SCHOOL NURSE
SCHOOL COUNSELLOR
POLICE OFFICER
MEALS SUPERVISOR
SCHOOL CARETAKER
SCHOOL BUS DRIVER
HEALTH PROMOTION UNIT
EDUCATIONAL PSYCHOLOGIST
EDUCATION WELFARE OFFICER
LOCAL COUNCILLOR
MP
NEIGHBOUR
RELIGIOUS LEADER

TACKLING BULLYING IN OUR SCHOOL/INSTITUTION: *Exercise*

Object: To gather specific information about your own school/institution, such as which areas need more supervision and which students might be bullies and/or victims

Time: 45 minutes

Materials: Paper and pens

In small groups the participants should address the following concerns and make lists:

1. What are the areas in the school which are most likely to need monitoring?
2. What are the crucial times when bullying might occur?
3. Which children/young people are most likely to be involved in bullying others?
4. Which children/young people are most likely to be influenced by the bullies into bullying behaviour?
5. Which children/young people are most likely to be or become victims?
6. Are racial and gender issues likely to be a part of the bullying pattern in your school/institution? If so, please list how they have been or might be involved.
7. Which children/young people do you think are the most positive influence within the school/institution? How could you use their influence to help the victims/bullies?

It is particularly useful to do this exercise *before* looking at the results of the anonymous Questionnaire (See WHY USE A QUESTIONNAIRE later in this SECTION). Although the students' Questionnaires may not give you the names of other pupils, they will pinpoint when and where they think bullying is happening. How can you use this combined information to improve your school/institution's atmosphere and safety?

Information received at the Parents' Meeting will help complete the picture (see WHY INFORM PARENTS? later in this SECTION).

1

When you have gathered the information, use it to work out a plan of action including:

*   which places you will monitor

*   when you will monitor

*   which students you will try to supervise/help

*   how you will use the postitive influences in the school/institution to counteract or prevent bullying

These ideas will also help you set up your whole-school/institution anti-bullying policy (see PRODUCING AN ANTI-BULLYING POLICY later in this SECTION).

FOLLOW-UP EXERCISE:

Make a list of the people who might help tackle bullying and brainstorm all the things they could do:

Teaching Staff

Pastoral Staff

Students

Dinner Supervisors

Playground Supervisors

Parents

Outside Agencies

(see also ROLES OVERHEAD in the previous Exercise)

WHY USE A QUESTIONNAIRE?: *Course Notes*

One of the most effective ways of establishing exactly how big a problem bullying is within a particular group is to ask students to complete a Survey Questionnaire on the nature and frequency of bullying within their school/institution. This will give precise information about bullying which can then be incorporated in the final anti-bullying policy. (For example, if one of the answers to the questions Where and When does bullying most frequently take place, is 'the toilets after lunch', staff supervision in the toilets at this time ought to reduce this particular problem.)

Many schools without anti-bullying policies have told KIDSCAPE that they 'didn't have any bullying'. Then they have set the questionnaire which has revealed that not only do they have bullying but that it is extensive and occurs throughout the school.

The Questionnaire should be designed to discover

* *who* bullies,
* *where* bullying takes place
* *when* bullying occurs
* *what* form the bullying takes.

The Questionnaire will also reveal some of the students' feelings about bullying and whether they are interested in tackling the problem.

The next Exercise DEVISING A QUESTIONNAIRE gives practical information on how to draw up a Questionnaire appropriate for your school/organization.

HOW TO USE THE QUESTIONNAIRE

Appoint a Staff Co-ordinator or a small group of staff volunteers to devise the Questionnaire with the help of colleagues and students. Some schools also include parents in this process, which helps to eliminate any future misunderstandings.

Alternately, you can use the Questionnaires provided in this manual or adapt them to suit your own organisation.

Send home copies of the Questionnaire to parents so they will know what is happening (see THE PARENT'S LETTER later in this SECTION).

Distribute copies to every child in the school and have them complete the Questionnaires in class. It is best if the students fill out their Questionnaires anonymously as they will then be more likely to answer honestly. Sometimes children are worried that their handwriting will be recognised. To overcome this, the Questionnaire might be couched in such a way that children can tick boxes, rather than writing full answers. This will obviously depend upon the age and abilities of the children. With some children it will be necessary to help them fill in the questions or perhaps meet each child or young person individually.

Once all the Questionnaires have been completed, the Co-ordinator should compile a summary for the staff, (or each teachers could compile a summary for their class/year which the Co-ordinator could collate). This summary should then be distributed to the whole staff, including meals and playground supervisors, so that everyone knows what and where the problems are.

Some schools ask students to fill in the same Questionnaire every year. As the anti-bullying policy takes effect, the answers to the questions will change (for example, more pupils will be prepared to tell about bullying once they realise that victims will be protected). Comparing the results from successive years provides a simple way of measuring the success of the anti-bullying policy.

SPECIMEN QUESTIONNAIRES

Two specimen Questionnaires are included (after the next Exercise): one from Teenscape by Michele Elliott aimed at adolescents and one for very young children from the KIDSCAPE Primary Child Protection Programme. These are included as examples which serve to illustrate the general principles involved but we think the most effective Questionnaires are those which are 'home-grown' and specifically designed with a particular school/institution in mind. The Questionnaire then suits individual circumstances.

DEVISING A QUESTIONNAIRE: *Exercise*

Object: This Exercise helps participants devise a questionnaire which they can use in their own schools/institutions

Time: 20 - 30 minutes

Show OVERHEAD/HANDOUT: WHY DO A QUESTIONNAIRE?
Ask participants to break into small groups and ask each group to devise a survey on bullying in the form of a questionnaire.

The Questionnaire should be designed to discover

* who bullies,
* where bullying takes place
* when bullying occurs
* what form the bullying takes.

Ask the groups for their feedback. Was the Exercise difficult? Why?

Did anyone include questions about teachers who bully? (This can often be very sensitive as usually everyone knows which members of staff are bullies but no one seems prepared to tell them so. You could include a question about which teachers bully but be prepared for civil war in the staff room!)

You can use the Questionnaires produced by the different groups as a basis for devising the Questionnaire for use in your school/ organisation.

One word of advice is not to let the whole process or the Questionnaire itself become too long or too complicated. Set a time limit and try to stick to it.

WHY DO A QUESTIONNAIRE?

To find out:

* * If bullying is taking place

* * If students are interested or concerned

* * Where it is happening

* * Time that it is happening

* * Patterns of bullying

* * Student feelings about bullying

SPECIMEN QUESTIONNAIRES – Young Children & Teens

The following questionnaire for young children is from the KIDSCAPE Primary Child Protection Programme:

Questionnaire for Young Children:

Ask the children to fill in the blank with drawings or with happy or sad faces or words. You will obviously have to help some of the children – this is a good opportunity to find out if bullying is going on and where:

Who makes you happy?

Does anyone make you unhappy?

Draw a happy or a sad face: ☺ ☹

Are you happy or unhappy:

Playground   Classroom

Toilets   Lunchroom

Coming to school   Going home from school

1

The following questionnaire has been adapted from TEENSCAPE: A Personal Safety Programme for Teenagers by M. Elliott, Health Education Authority, 1995 (available from KIDSCAPE):

Teenscape Questionnaire about Bullying

a) Have you ever been bullied?

_____yes   _____no

b) At what age?

_____under five   _____5-11   _____11-14   _____Over 14

c) Did/do you consider the bullying to have been

_____no problem   _____worrying   _____frightening

_____so bad that you didn't want to go out or to school

d) Did the bullying

_____have no effect   _____some bad effect

_____terrible effect   _____make you change your life in
some way (e.g. change schools)

e) Is the bullying still happening?

_____yes   _____no

f)   If the bullying is still happening, where is it occurring?

_____classroom   _____during sports   _____toilets

_____after school   _____lunchroom   _____halls

_____library   _____activities   _____everywhere

g) How often is the bullying happening?

_____very seldom   _____once a day

_____once a month   _____several times a day

_____once a week

h) Is the bullying

_____physical   _____verbal   _____racial

_____sexual   _____emotional (being sent to
                                       Coventry/ignored etc)

_____threats   _____taking possessions/money

i) Do you know anyone who is being bullied, but has not told?

_____yes   _____no

j) Please tick if you are a _____girl   _____boy

k) Was the bully (bullies)

_____a girl   ____a boy   ___both

_____a gang   ____teacher   ____member of staff

l) If you were or are being bullied, have you ever told anyone?

_____yes   _____no

m) Did the bullying stop when you told?

_____yes   _____no

n) Did the bullying become worse because you told?

_____yes   _____no

o) Have you ever bullied anyone? _____yes   _____no

p) Are you bullying someone in this school now? ___yes   __no

q) What should be done about the problem of bullying?

_____

_____

_____

_____

WHY INFORM PARENTS?: *Course Notes*

It seems a very good idea to grab the interest of parents right at the start of the school year. This is the ideal time for meetings and communications about possible problems – before they actually arise so that no one feels defensive.

Eric Jones, teacher and Deputy Head, suggests: 'A meeting of all parents, early in the life of their children at any school, can help us avoid losing their sympathies and prevent anyone's heels becoming dug in on a particular issue. In the midst of trumpeting how marvellous the library is and how wonderful the staff and students are, go in hard with the point that children make mistakes, do nasty things and that you will need the parents' help all along the way. Mention the difficulties which can arise when parents (and teachers and students) rampage without listening to both sides of a story. Gain their trust before the rot sets in!'

Then, when you do a Survey using a Questionnaire about bullying, it will not seem that this is something arising out of panic or that your school is the 'bullying capital' of the world. Do try to involve parents in making up the questionnaire.

Before giving the students the Survey/Questionnaire, it is a good idea to write to all parents to let them know that the school is planning to introduce a positive whole-school anti-bullying policy. In the past, the reputation of some schools has suffered as parents have mistakenly assumed that because the school was tackling bullying, it must therefore have a major bullying problem. This is an unfortunate but common misconception and a letter setting out the school's strategy for eliminating bulllying will clarify the situation, reassure parents and prevent the switchboard lighting up with 100 telephone calls!

A draft letter is included for information. Enclose a copy of the Questionnaire with the letter so that parents can see exactly what questions their children will be asked.

Make sure that the school governors and the PTA are kept fully informed of the anti-bullying initiative from the beginning.

It is a good idea to arrange a Parent/Teacher Meeting so that parents can ask questions and staff have an opportunity to explain exactly what the new anti-bullying policy will mean for pupils, teachers, parents and others involved with the school (Governors, meals supervisors, playground supervisors, etc).

Draft letter to parents:

Dear

There has been much national media attention focused on the problem of bullying. As far as we are aware, our school does not have a particular problem with bullying, but we would like to ensure that this is the case. We know that children and young people learn better when they are happy and not worried.

Having talked to the students,* we have decided that an anonymous survey questionnaire about bullying would be helpful. We will be giving the students the enclosed Questionnaire and thought that you would appreciate seeing a copy. We will be grateful for your support. We are giving the students the Questionnaire on .... and we will keep you informed of the results.

If you have any questions, there will be a brief Meeting for Parents on.......................... We should be very grateful if you would keep any questions until this Meeting as we are so busy at the moment with the start of the school year.

Thank you again for your support.

Yours sincerely,

* Note: If you have had parents involved from the start of this process it would be helpful to say: Having involved students, staff and parents, we have decided etc.

SCHOOL CONTRACTS: *Course Notes*

Although we refer to a School Contract thoroughout these Notes, the principles can be applied to any institution.

WHAT IS A SCHOOL CONTRACT?

School Contracts are sometimes called Equal Opportunities Statements. They define acceptable standards of behaviour between individuals and they make clear exactly what is expected of students. They create an ethos which encourages all individuals to develop to their full potential and which encourages racial and cultural pride along with a commitment to the overall good of the school community. They make it clear that victimising others for whatever reason will not be tolerated and that all incidents of bullying will be followed up.

A carefully devised Contract means that everybody knows what they can and cannot do. Nobody can say "I didn't know it wasn't allowed". If bullying takes place, victims know that they can tell and bullies know that they will not be able to depend on the silence of victims or witnesses for protection. Nobody 'gets away with anything'.

The term 'School Contract' is preferred by most workshop participants to terms like 'School Rules' because the Contract is drawn up after serious consultation with students. Contracts are not just imposed arbitrarily upon the student body; they are discussed and amended, and the final version is the result of agreement between all members of the school.

Schools may have several supporting policies, for example a Discipline Policy, an Equal Opportunities policy and an Anti-Bullying Policy: each complementing the others and together defining the school's outlook.

WHY HAVE A SCHOOL CONTRACT?

* a written contract means that everybody knows exactly what is expected of them
* contracts provide clear simple guidelines
* contracts eliminate "I didn't know it wasn't allowed" excuses
* nobody 'gets away with anything'
* students from different racial and cultural backgrounds are not victimised
* sexual harassment is outlawed
* contracts teach students how to behave as responsible members of a community
* involving students in drawing up and revising the contract when necessary means that they 'own' it and it reflects their concerns
* as acceptable behaviour is clearly set out, it is much easier to identify when students are behaving unacceptably

HOW TO DEVISE A SCHOOL CONTRACT

* Appoint one member of staff or a small group of volunteers to co-ordinate the project and to collate the answers.

* Initiate a series of class discussion projects in which each class is asked to come up with five or ten 'rules of behaviour'.

These class projects can be used to stimulate discussion about bullying and about the sort of behaviour which is acceptable between individuals and groups. They help raise awareness about bullying. (National Curriculum: cross-curricular Education or Citizenship theme).

* From the suggestions put forward, it should be possible to draw up a Contract which includes most of the students' ideas.

* When the draft Contract is drawn up, students, staff, parents, meals supervisors and others should be made aware of its contents and asked for their comments.

WAYS TO USE THE CONTRACT

* The final version of the Contract could be distributed to every student or included in the student handbook, if you have one.

* Ask each student and their parents to sign a copy of the Contract. This can be placed in the student's file. (If the Contracts are printed on coloured paper, they are easily visible and no one can then say they signed by mistake!)

* Display copies in classrooms, and/or in the corridors and main hall. You may wish to put the Contract into a plastic case so it cannot be defaced, depending upon the circumstances of your school or institution.

* Include a copy of the Contract in the parent's booklet or handbook, if you have one, or send a copy home.

* Read it to each class at the beginning of term. Go over the Contract with new pupils.

Two Specimen Contracts are included as examples. The first example was devised by pupils and the second by teachers.

1

Note: As with everything else, there has to be a balance between enthusiasm and the practicality of school/institution life. Bullying is obviously not the only issue on the agenda: schedules, rosters, lunch and break arrangements, anti-racism and equal opportunities policies, homework policies and all sorts of other things will often also need to be displayed. Displaying only the Anti-Bullying Policy or the School Contract may lead visitors to conclude that bullying is rife! If possible, include a variety of issues in the Contract - all of which apply to most schools and institutions, such as everyone taking responsibility within the school, no littering or vandalism, acceptance of others etc.

The Contract could include your anti-racism and equal opportunities policies, thus eliminating another piece of paper to display. The Contract could also be included in the school diary (if you have one) and in the booklet often given to parents explaining how the school operates. Since the Contract will probably be renewed or revised each year, you may wish to put a notation on the contract of the year or term it covers.

FIRST SPECIMEN CONTRACT

1. We will not tolerate bullying or harassing of any kind.

2. We will be accepting of others regardless or race, religion, culture or disabilities.

3. We will not pass by if we see anyone being bullied – we will either try to stop it or go for help.

4. We will not allow bullying or harassing going to or from school, either on the school bus or public transport or walking.

5. We will allow a quiet area in the playground for those who do not want to run around or play games.

6. We will use our 'time out' room if we feel angry or under pressure or just need time to calm down or work out what is wrong.

7. We will not litter or draw on school property (walls, books, toilets, desks, etc).

8. We will be kind to others, even if they are not our friends and we will make new students feel welcome.

9. On school journeys we will act in a way which brings credit to our school.

10. We will be honest about anything we have done or are supposed to have done.

11. We will have a discussion group once a week in class to talk about any problems that are bothering us.

12. We will participate in the school council and we will abide by its decisions.

SECOND SPECIMEN CONTRACT

1. We will behave sensibly and with consideration for others when we are in school.

2. We will take turns in a queue.

3. We will not interfere with other people's property and we will not bring precious things to school.

4. We will not pick on other students.

5. We will listen to and respect other people's opinions.

6. We will report any bullying incident to a member of staff.

7. Staff and students will talk politely to each other and will give each other a fair hearing.

8. We should have a quiet, supervised area to go to away from others.

9. We will be willing to help other students if necessary.

10. Staff will supervise 'trouble spots'.

11. We will not join in fights or disturbances but will immediately report them to a member of staff.

12. We will make the playground a fun place to be with enough things to do (inside too for wet days).

13. We will look after new students.

14. We will not judge others on their appearance or the way they speak.

15. We will put ourselves in others people's shoes.

16. We will not put other people down.

17. We will look for people's good points.

18. We will try to remember that everyone matters – including ourselves.

SCHOOL CONTRACTS: *Exercise*

Object: To encourage participants to focus on the most important points which should be contained in a contract acceptable to all those involved with the school

Time: 45 minutes

Ask participants to form groups and ask each group to come up with ten points for inclusion in a School Contract. After 30 minutes ask one member of each group to explain the point their group thought most important.

These points might form the basis of a School Contract.

Show OVERHEAD/HANDOUT: KIDSCAPE CONTRACTS.
After hearing the feedback from the different groups, you could give them copies of the Specimen Contracts (see previous item on School Contracts)
Ask the groups to decide which Contract was devised by students and which by teachers. The *First* Specimen Contract was devised by students – this usually comes as a surprise to participants!

1

KIDSCAPE CONTRACTS

* Clear, simple guidelines

* Devised by students and staff

* School copy can be displayed for all to see

and/or

* Individual copies can be signed by or given to each student and parent

* Each student can sign a copy, which is then kept in student file

* This signed copy eliminates 'I didn't know' excuse

CONSEQUENCES

Once you have drawn-up a Contract which outlaws bullying, you need to consider what happens when pupils infringe its anti-bullying provisions. Very often, after classroom discussions, role-play, drawing-up and signing the Contract, the students themselves will ensure that bullying doesn't take place. However, peer pressure might not be enough in itself to eradicate bullying and it is therefore important that everyone should know exactly what will happen if bullying continues to take place.

TELLING

As part of the whole school policy, encourage children to tell about bullying. Eric Jones suggests that we explain to students that:

* **Telling is an obligation.** There is nothing shameful in it. Staff have a right to know about incidents. Victims and bystanders have an obligation and duty to tell. If they do not, then they are giving the bully tacit permission to continue bullying the victim and others with impunity. It is important that we burst the bully's bubble of silence and blow his or her cover. It's secrecy which allows bullying to flourish – once bullies discover that they cannot rely on the silence of victims and bystanders, they realise that they won't be able to 'get away with it' any longer.

* **Telling is not grassing.** Forget it! Grassing is when you are involved in an incident and you tell on your cronies when you get caught (not that there is necessarily anything the matter with that). Telling is what you do and must do when you are the sought-out victim or when something happens to you. It is also what you do when you see someone else as the victim. It is not grassing – it is an obligation. Not telling is tantamount to involvement, conniving or condoning.

This is an important message to get across to children, especially since many may have been taught that telling and asking for help is a sign of weakness. *Teach children that you expect them to report any bullying*, whether as victim or as a witness. Once bullies know that their actions will be reported *automatically*, they quickly learn that they can no longer rely on the silence of victim and bystanders to protect them.

1

REPORTING INCIDENTS

You need to set up an efficient system of reporting incidents so that action can be taken. Everybody, especially new pupils, needs to understand how the system works and how bullying incidents should be reported.

Set out the procedure for reporting incidents and ensure that all students are either given a copy or that the procedure is posted in several places where students can read it. Remind pupils at the beginning of each term of the procedure for reporting bullying incidents, perhaps at a school assembly or in class meetings.

In setting this procedure up, keep in mind that you need to beware the crisis or panic response. An incident may be important but it is not always a crisis which needs immediate action. A boy with his trousers on fire – that is a crisis. A child attempting suicide or threatening suicide – that is a crisis. Someone taking someone else's ball on the playground needs action, but perhaps not immediately. It is important that parents and students understand that it is not always possible to spring into action straight away, though the incident will be dealt with as soon as humanly possible.

The procedure set out below is given as an example only. Each school or institution will want to devise their own scheme to fit their own particular circumstances. Of course, the best way forward is for children to feel comfortable about telling, but initially you may wish to set up an anonymous way for children to tell. You can move away from this when the students feel more confident about telling staff face to face.

1. Set up an 'Incidents Box' where pupils can 'post' notes about what has happened and/or other worries they may have. In one Incidents Box, a student expressed the fear that a friend was thinking of killing herself. It turned out to be true and a potential tragedy was averted. (In Marston Middle School in Oxford they set up the box as an initial approach. The very existence of the 'Incidents Box' was enough of a deterrent and the small amount of bullying which was happening ceased virtually overnight).

As every teacher knows, this does not mean that every report will be honest – there is always the possibility of malicious intent. However, in most schools and institutions using the Incidents Box, it has been responsibly used. The real difficulty it that it does create more work for the staff.

2. Empty the box every day – this should be done by the member of staff appointed as policy co-ordinator. In the real world this might prove to be difficult, but the amount of reports do decrease after the initial rush!

WAYS OF DEALING WITH REPORTS OF INCIDENTS

3. The reports posted in the Incidents Box can be given to the class teacher/year head/class or school meeting depending on the agreed reporting system. The member of staff/meeting talks to the victim and then sees the bully/bullies (gang members should be interviewed separately). The member of staff/meeting decides what action should be taken.

4. A brief summary of the incident (see Specimen Incident Report at the end of this item) should be filed in one place to provide an accurate record of bullying, perhaps in a Bullying Book kept especially for this purpose (in one school this is known as the Red Book and 'being put into the Red Book' is a recognised deterrent). More serious incidents and all those involving physical assault, or racial or sexual bullying, should be reported to the Head Teacher.

A copy of the Incident Report may then be placed in the victim's and bully's files. If the bully does not re-offend within an agreed time, the copies in the files could be destroyed and the name of the bully erased or Tipp-Exed out of the Bullying Book (to keep an accurate record of incidents, you may wish to leave the incident on file).

However, if bullying happens again, parents could be asked to come into school for a meeting with the Head Teacher and Year Head/Class Teacher, or another course of action could be taken, such as the bully having privileges removed.

An advantage of maintaining a Bully Book is that it can show the decline in levels of bullying at your school or institution and can be shown (without individual names) as a record of an effective anti-bullying policy.

GETTING OUTSIDE HELP

5. It may sometimes be necessary to get outside help (education welfare officer/child psychologist) to deal with persistent bullies and regular victims. This is, of course, done after the bully or victim and their family have been informed and, whenever possible, involved in helping the bully or victim.

SPECIMEN INCIDENT REPORT

A sample of an incident report is provided here. Whatever you decide to use, it should be easily recognisable and simple to complete – everyone has enough to do without filling in miles and miles of extra paperwork. One simple way to recognise the reports in a file or in a busy office would be to colour code them – one colour for 'bad' incidents, another colour for 'good' reports. That is if your budget will stretch that far.

Eric Jones suggests that we should not 'pull any punches' about recording incidents. It is quite effective to say to someone who has been bullying that: 'This is on the record. If you never do anything like it again, there is no need to worry. However, if you continue to behave like this then we have on record when it all began. You have been warned.' Then you can decide whether to destroy the report or keep it in the file – this will depend upon what your school or institutional policy is. Some people think the culprit should be given a chance for a completely clean start by taking the Incident Report out of the file if the bully is a reformed character. Others feel it should be left, but ignored if the bully doesn't re-offend and has learned his/her lesson.

You may wish to have the bully and victim write down their accounts and attached them to the Incident Report.

INCIDENT REPORT SHEET

Date ....

Details of incident ....

....

....

Action taken and Date ....

....

....

Follow-up action necessary? ....

....

Victim informed of action ....

Other staff members informed ....

Signature of member of staff ....

Seen by Head Teacher ....

* Statements attached from ....

....

....

Successful intervention is rooted in an effective whole-school anti-bullying policy which has a clear code of conduct. Reporting incidents is also vital – all students must understand that if they bully, they will be reported. They must also understand that bullying, however 'minor' or 'trivial' the incident, will not be ignored. ALL reports of bullying will be followed up.

It is important to deal with the immediate fall-out from the bullying incident as quickly as possible, given all the other constraints on staff time. Delay can be interpreted by bullies as hesitation on the part of the staff and this can undermine the positive message that bullying will not be tolerated. However, as we have said before in this Guide, crisis incidents will obviously take priority, with other incidents being handled as soon as possible.

The response to bullying incidents should be carefully thought out (see previous COURSE NOTES: AFTER THE CONTRACT) and should be known and understood throughout the school.

Don't get too bogged down in too many details – try to keep the investigation simple. But if you listen to one side of the story, it is important to listen to the other side. Failure to listen carefully may cause us to miss out the very real problems which all parties may have, and, worse, can be interpreted as refusing to be impartial.

JUST AND ONLY

Just and only are often key words used by bullies to defend their behaviour. They are used to diminish the seriousness of whatever has happened. They occur in sentences like:

"I *only* pushed her"; "I *just* hit him once"; "We were *only* teasing".

From the victim's point of view they were pushed, or hit – only and just are irrelevant.

One enlightened Headteacher, Linda Frost, has banned the words only and just from all explanations. This means that admissions like "I only pushed her", "I just kicked her once", change to "I pushed her", "I kicked her once."

A GAME, A JOKE, AN ACCIDENT

Teachers are often told, by way of excuse, "It was a game", or "It was a joke", or "It was an accident". To find out if it really was a game, a joke or an accident, Eric Jones, speaking at the KIDSCAPE First National Conference on Bullying in 1989, suggested asking the following questions when faced with excuses such as, "It was a game", "It was a joke", "It was an accident":

"*It was a game*": Did everyone join in? Was anybody left out? Did they want to be left out? Was everyone happy to play? If it really was a game as alleged, then everyone should have been happy to play and those not playing would have chosen not to join in.

"*It was a joke*": Was everyone laughing? Did everyone find it funny? If it really was a joke as alleged, then everyone should be amused.

"*It was an accident*": Has someone gone to fetch help? Has anyone apologised? Is anyone comforting the person who has been hurt? This is what happens after a real accident. If it's not happening, then whatever happened was not an 'accident'.

Sometimes excuses can be bizarre: one mother, when told her daughter had been fighting other girls, turned to the culprit and asked her "Now, did you hit them in a nice or a nasty way?" When in doubt, find out who has been hurt and go from there!

Eric Jones also suggests that schools introduce rules about borrowing, such as banning it altogether to avoid victims being coerced into agreeing with the bully that the disputed item was 'borrowed'. If borrowing is not allowed, then another 'bully haven' is eradicated.

The object of not accepting these lame excuses is to get the bullies to own up to what they have done and not to rationalise away the pain they have caused others. Otherwise the bully's behaviour will not change and the excuses will go on and on.

ACTION PLAN

The following steps are given as a general guide and will generally be applicable to most incidents. However, individual schools and organizations will want to include their own particular requirements.

* If you witness the bullying, the first thing to do is stop it and remove the bully from the situation – some schools have instituted special 'time-out' areas for bullies, somewhere they can go and cool off.

* Reassure the victim that they will be protected and the bullying will be stopped. If the victim has come forward and told you about a bullying incident or about a series of incidents, praise them for telling.

* If the victim is hurt, seek medical attention.

* If there are bruises or cuts, it might be useful to take pictures so that later denials of harm can be dealt with quickly.

* Get the bully to think of ways to atone for his/her actions – insist on compensation for items lost, damaged or stolen, the return of items 'borrowed' or stolen, and the repayment of money stolen.

* Try to get the bully to apologise to the victim – the bully may not 'feel' sorry and there may not be genuine remorse at this stage. Accept even the most grudging apology, but work towards teaching the bully and other children *how* to apologise. In some families, the concept is completely foreign because someone else is always blamed. We want to teach the bully that hurting people either physically or emotionally is wrong and that when you have hurt someone you have to acknowledge the fact both to yourself and to the person you have hurt. Saying sorry is the first step for the bully towards recognising that their bullying behaviour is wrong. In some cases this might be a losing battle and the apology may have to come at a later stage, but it is worth trying.

* Set in motion the agreed school procedures for dealing with bullying incidents and with bullies (entering them in the Bully Book/reporting to Class Meeting or Student Council)

* If the bullying involves squabbling between friends or minor incidents between generally well-motivated children, it may be possible to sort the situation out by sitting down with victim and bully and getting them to talk about what happened and why. A round discussion gives all parties an opportunity to air any grievances and to say how they feel (see the next COURSE NOTES: 'COMMON CONCERN APPROACH'). Minor incidents can often be resolved in this way. (Such a discussion might take place during a class meeting if appropriate.)

* If appropriate, sanctions relating to the most recent incident might be imposed by the class teacher or member of staff responsible for the bullying policy or for the Student Council.

It is important that bullies realise that aggressive, violent, or cruel behaviour is unacceptable and that if they act in this way they will face unpleasant consequences. Sanctions need not be draconian, but they should be effective. Some sanctions which have worked are listed below.

* If assault or theft are involved, it may be necessary to involve the police. The parents of the victim will need to be consulted – some will not press charges and will not be happy if the police are called without their knowledge. You may wish to talk to the local School Liaison Officer or the Community Liaison Officer about 'having a chat' in the Headteacher's office to the bully involved. Even if charges are not pressed, the bully will have learned that the school is serious about eradicating bullying and view it as totally unacceptable. (Two of the inmates in the Young Offender Institutions which took part in the KIDSCAPE survey had been victims of bullying at school and they told us that it was the threat of police action which finally stopped the bullying.)

SANCTIONS WHICH HAVE WORKED

* writing bully's name in a Bullying Book

* a report in the bully's file, a letter home and a meeting between parents and the school

* the bully has to account for his/her actions to a student or class meeting, or to a committee of the student council

* assigning a senior pupil to monitor the bully – the bully cannot go into the playground or around the school without the senior pupil

* assigning the bully to assist a particular member of staff with special tasks at break times

* keep the bully in during breaks, perhaps sitting in the Headteacher's office, or in another room where supervision is available

* the bully has to do his/ her work in a room alone for a day/a week

* the bully is kept behind to allow the other children to go home unmolested, if the bully is bothering children after school or on their way to and from school

* photographing the bully's actions so s/he can see what you are talking about without the excuse of 'I didn't do it'

* the bully eats lunch at a separate table from other students, or has to sit next to a staff member, or has to eat in another supervised room

* the bully is assigned extra duties: clearing and scraping the plates after meals, sorting and stacking books in the library, checking cloakrooms at the end of the day. (Make sure that the bully is praised for accomplishing these duties well.)

* one primary school, which suffered from children kicking each other, decided that a child caught kicking would have his/her shoes removed for the day. The shoeless bully then had to remain inside all day and the bully's shoes had to be collected by parents from the staff room at the end of the day (Be cautious about this – it could be construed as child abuse!)

* in one school, the pupils decided that a particular bully was not allowed to wear fashionable trainers – the bully's credibility was destroyed instantly when he had to appear in ordinary shoes!

* Eric Jones, who has had years of experience as a Deputy Head and classroom teacher, says not to forget that the 'good old fashioned telling-off, done formally, without interruption, and then put on record' can be very effective. He warns that what is said should not be sarcastic, vengeful or personally insulting, but should state facts about unacceptable behaviour and consequences to actions. 'It should point towards the future, hoping for something better, expecting something better' and then 'the incident put behind us with the culprit being given a chance to prove him/herself or otherwise'.

* ultimately, if all else fails and the bullying continues, it may be necessary to suspend the bully from school for a period

The message to get across to the bully is that the consequences of persisting with unacceptable behaviour could well be unpleasant and that it is better to abide by the provisions of the School Contract. If the bully does improve, then there could be rewards instead of sanctions.

See also the EXERCISE: SUGGESTIONS WHICH WORK

The main points in this Section are summarized in the following Overheads for groupwork.

INTERVENTION: IMMEDIATE ACTION

* **SET CLEAR EXPECTATIONS**
School Contract
Bullying will NEVER be ignored

* **EXPLAIN CONSEQUENCES**
Everyone should know what will happen if bullying continues

* **STOP THE BULLYING**

* **REMOVE BULLY** to cool down
Have a time-out place for bullies

* **REASSURE VICTIMS**

* **APOLOGY TO VICTIM**

* **FIND BULLY WAYS TO ATONE**

* **SET IN MOTION SCHOOL'S AGREED ANTI-BULLYING PROCEDURES**

* **SANCTIONS** if appropriate

Beware the joke ...

that isn't funny

Beware the game ...

the victim wasn't playing

Beware the accident ...

that wasn't an accident ...

and wasn't treated as such

Beware the loan ...

exacted under duress

Ban borrowing and lending

COMMON CONCERN: *Course Notes*

Anatol Pikas, Professor of Psychology at Uppsala University, has pioneered what he calls 'the common concern approach' for tackling bullying. Using this method, children are brought together to try to work out a mutually agreeable way to deal with bullying.

Professor Pikas says that the purpose is to get the children who are bullying to arrive at a common feeling of concern for the victim(s) and to use this concern to change behaviour and to develop empathy. This method can be quite successful when dealing with groups of children who have previously been friends and have fallen out or with children who have not turned to sustained vicious or violent bullying. It is more difficult if the bullies are picking on children they don't know or care about and if the patterns of bullying are so well established that the bullying itself has become a reward for the bullies.

The Pikas method is based on a treatment model and the assumption that each member of the bullying group wants the bullying to stop. The adult who is intervening avoids blaming anyone or arguing about facts. Pikas recommends that the bully gang be interviewed separately, with the adult 'therapist' using five steps:

Step One – Low-key start
'I would like to talk with you because I've heard that you've been bothering John.'

Step Two – Agreement
'What do you know about it?'

Step Three – Going Forward – No Recriminations
'All right, we've talked about it long enough for now.'

Step Four – Solving it
'What to do? What do you suggest?'

Step Five – Trusting the Bully
That's good. We'll meet again in a week and you can tell me how you've been getting on.'

According to Pikas, the most important intervention is between Steps two and three. 'Beginners often believe that at the second point the suspected mobber (bully) would answer with 'Nothing!' In fact, most bullies want to talk about the situation. The task of the adult is to reinforce the bully's answers with comments and further questions in such a way that the dialogue works towards the idea that the victim's situation is something to be concerned about.' *

The aim of the interview is for the adult 'therapist' and the bully to become partners sharing a common concern to put the situation right.

This method does take time and careful planning, but it can pay dividends when working with many cases of bullying and especially with groups of friends who may turn on one another.

A similar counselling technique called the 'no blame approach' which is based on the common concern method has been used in some UK schools. (See BOOKS AND VIDEOS FOR PROFESSIONALS at the end of this Guide).

* The Common Concern Method for the Treatment of Mobbing by Anatol Pikas in Bullying, An International Perspective edited by Erling Roland & Elaine Munthe, David Fulton Publishers, 1989

SUGGESTIONS WHICH WORK!: *Exercise*

Object: To share ideas which have worked to stop or prevent bullying in schools/institutions

Time: 10 minutes to 30 minutes

Materials: Paper and pens

Ask the participants to break into small groups and discuss ideas which have worked for them, or ideas they have heard about, or which they think might work. Give them as much time as necessary and then meet in the large group to talk about the results. Participants on KIDSCAPE courses often rate this as one of the most helpful activities. They have contributed some of the following ideas:

Create a safe space for anyone who wishes to use it

Put up a suggestion box for the students for all kinds of suggestions (if it is just about bullying you may find children reluctant to go near it)

Hold class meetings/bully courts

Assign an older 'friend' or 'pilot' to all new children – this often prevents older students picking on younger ones

Time out place for bullies to get their frustration or anger under control

Change the Seating – sometimes students exclude others because they are always allowed to sit with friends and never think to include other students. Tell the students at the beginning of the term that they will be assigned to seats for three days of the week and allowed to sit where they like the other two days. This allows you some flexibility to change the seating several times (perhaps once a month) to ensure that some students aren't always left out and gives the students a chance to get to know people outside their groups.

Kindness campaign – have a week in which people are nominated for acts of kindness and give recognition in the form of certificates or prizes

Poster contest – have the students design anti-bullying posters and ask a local celebrity to judge and give awards. Tell the local press and get some good publicity

KIDSCAPE programmes – use the Under Fives, Primary and Teenscape programmes in school. They all deal with bullying

Art project – have the students design a mural, sculpture or another art project around the theme of bullying

Drama project – ask the students to write and produce a play about bullying

Student Helpers/Counsellors – train some older responsible students to help other students with problems like bullying. Often young people will talk to each other when they won't seek adult help, so student counsellors could be a first contact. The important point here is that the students need time, a place and adult guidance and support to do this. It is essential, too, that they know what their limits are (for example, if someone tells them about abuse, they will have to understand that they should not be expected to keep that confidential).

Weekly assemblies re bullying presented by different classes

Letter home to parents explaining all the things you are doing to prevent bullying

Contracts with students regarding conduct kept on coloured paper in file (so that it is easy to find it amongst the other papers)

Use photographs – some schools have taken photos of children in the playground and then used these to talk to the children about bullying. If the school cannot afford a camera, it is possible to pretend that you have one trained on the playground. In one school, they had a camera, but no film. The teachers 'took' photos in an obvious manner anyway and that was enough to stop the bullying. Very few bullies want to have their exploits recorded.

One mother followed her child to school at a distance using a video camera to record the bullying which the bullies had previously denied. She then invited the parents of the children over to view the video – the bullying stopped immediately! (How on earth she managed to film without coming out of the bushes to confront the bully, we'll never know)

Lessons about issues, such as grief, race, divorce, special needs – these help students to understand what others might be going through and could eliminate some causes of bullying

Keep a 'journal' about bullying – a fact/fiction journal for English raises interesting discussion (see Teenscape for an example)

Hold a debate about the 'good' and 'bad' points about bullying

KIDSCAPE: How to stop bullying

Telling school – make your school a place where telling is the norm

No bystanders – make a school rules that there are no 'innocent bystanders' when it comes to bullying

Assertiveness training for all the children or young people

Ask a staff member to be available to bully and/or victim as a 'safety valve' (not a punching bag!)

Private help – ensure that there is a way to get help privately

See also SANCTIONS WHICH HAVE WORKED in IMMEDIATE ACTION – THE INCIDENT: COURSE NOTES

PRODUCING AN ANTI-BULLYING POLICY: Exercise

Object: To produce an anti-bullying policy

Time: 60 minutes

This Exercise can be done in several ways:

1) Break into small groups and ask each group to work on one particular phase of the policy

2) Break into small groups and ask each one to come up with a complete policy

3) Give each group a copy of the following KIDSCAPE anti-bullying policy and ask them either to agree with it or rewrite it

4) Look at your own anti-bullying policy and compare it with the following to determine if you are content with yours or would like to revise it in any way

If you are developing an anti-bullying policy from scratch, this Exercise may take several hours.

SPECIMEN KIDSCAPE ANTI-BULLYING POLICY:

We are committed to providing a caring, friendly and safe environment for all of our pupils so they can learn in a relaxed and secure atmosphere. Bullying of any kind is unacceptable at our school. If bullying does occur, all pupils should be able to tell and know that incidents will be deal with promptly and effectively. We are a TELLING school – anyone who knows that bullying is happening is expected to tell the staff.

WHAT IS BULLYING?

Bullying is the use of aggression with the intention of hurting another person, and which results in pain and distress to the victim.

Bullying can include:

Physical	pushing, kicking, hitting, pinching or any use of violence
Verbal	name-calling, sarcasm, spreading rumours, teasing
Emotional	excluding, tormenting (ie hiding books, threatening gestures), being unfriendly, racial taunts, graffiti, gestures
Sexual	unwanted physical contact or abusive comments

OBJECTIVES:

* All staff, governors, pupils and parents should have an understanding of bullying

* Bullying will not be tolerated

* Clear procedures for reporting bullying should be understood and followed

PROCEDURES and CONSEQUENCES

1. Report bullying incidents to staff

2. In cases of serious bullying, the incidents will be recorded by staff

3. Parents should be informed (in serious cases) and will be asked to come to a meeting to discuss the problem

4. If necessary and appropriate, police will be consulted

5. The bullying behaviour and threats of bullying must immediately stop

6. An attempt will be made to help the bully (bullies) change their behaviour

7. The bully will offer an apology and other appropriate consequences may take place

8. In serious cases, suspension or even exclusion will be considered

9. Whenever possible, the pupils will be reconciled

PREVENTION:

We will use KIDSCAPE methods for helping children to prevent bullying. As and when appropriate, this may include writing a set of school rules, signing a behaviour contract, writing stories or drawing pictures about bullying, reading stories about bullying or having them read to a class or assembly, making up roleplays (or using the KIDSCAPE roleplays) and having discussions about bullying.

1

SIGNS AND SYMPTOMS: (from KIDSCAPE Stop Bullying! booklet)

A child may indicate by signs or behaviour that he or she is being bullied. Adults should be aware that these are possible signs and that they should investigate if a child:

* is frightened of walking to or from school
* is unwilling to go to school
* begins to do poorly in school work
* becomes withdrawn, starts stammering
* regularly has books or clothes destroyed
* becomes distressed, stops eating
* cries easily, has nightmares
* becomes disruptive or aggressive
* has possessions go 'missing' & money 'lost'
* starts stealing money (to pay bully)
* is frightened to say what's wrong
* attempts suicide or runs away

These signs and behaviours could indicate other problems, but certainly bullying should be considered as a possibility and should be investigated.

HELP ORGANISATIONS:

Advisory Centre for Education (ACE)	0171 354 8321
ChildLine	0800 1111
Children's Legal Centre	0171 359 6251
Child Guidance Centre	See local directory
KIDSCAPE	0171 730 3300
Parentline	01268 757077

KIDSCAPE has three booklets about bullying:
* Stop Bullying!
* You Can Beat Bullying! A Guide for Young People
* Preventing Bullying: A Parent's Guide

For a free copy of each booklet send a large SAE to:
KIDSCAPE, 152 Buckingham Palace Road, London SW1W 9TR

INVOLVING PARENTS: *Course Notes and Draft Handouts*

When setting out the whole-school policy on bullying, remember that parents may appreciate some help in knowing how to get advice if their child is being bullied or even if their child is the one doing the bullying.

It is also important to find out what is going on in a child's life which might be contributing to the bullying. Parents are often in the best position to give schools/institutions important information which they would not otherwise know about.

You may wish to ask questions which will help clarify the situation:

QUESTIONS FOR PARENTS:

1. Has anything happened which could explain the bullying?

    * Has there been a change in the family living accommodation?

    * Has there been extra tension in the family lately for any reason?

    * Is there a new person living with the family – even temporarily? Is there a new lodger or house guest?

    * Has there been a birth, death, divorce or other event in the family?

2. What effect is the bullying having on the child or young person?

3. How long have they known about the bullying?

4. Have they talked to their child about his/her concerns and worries?

5. Have they approached the victim's/bully's family? What was the outcome?

6. Has anything like this happened in the past? How was it resolved?

7. Are there other children/young people or adults who are aware of what has happened or who have witnessed incidents who might be able to shed light on the situation?

8. What ideas have the parents for trying to sort out the problem?

1

ADVICE FOR PARENTS OF CHILDREN WHO ARE BEING BULLIED
(can be adapted for use as a Handout for Parents):

One KIDSCAPE workshop group suggested that parents be given a list such as:

If you are worried about your child:

1. Don't ignore problem

2. Encourage your child to talk to you about his/her feelings – tell your child you are always willing to listen

3. Try not to over-react, even if you are furious – it might frighten your child into silence and we want victims to talk, not retreat

4. Ask your child if s/he has any suggestions about changing the situation

5. Find out how fearful your child is and make sure that s/he feels protected

6. Take any threats of suicide or other desperate pleas seriously and seek help – better safe than sorry and children and young people sometimes go to extremes if they are miserable

7. Help your child develop a sense of humour and a way of 'throwing off' taunts (see SECTION 2: WORKING WITH BULLIES AND VICTIMS)

8. Praise your child, tell him/her how much you love and support them

9. Try to sort out the bullying at first as quietly and constructively as possible:

    * Contact class teacher

    * Try to give the situation time to change

    * If there is no improvement, contact the Headteacher

    * If you are still concerned, contact school governors – the school can tell you how to do this

    * If your child is still not being helped, then contact your Local Education Authority (LEA)

KIDSCAPE: How to stop bullying

* If you feel confident enough, you may wish to contact parents of the other child – that obviously depends upon the family of the bully. There are some families which bully not only their own children, but threaten anyone who comes near them – best to check out the situation carefully before getting involved.

10. Encourage your child to develop new interests which might lead to a supportive group of friends – in school and out of school. Saturday music clubs, church choir, sports activities, local drama groups, dancing/art/computer classes, martial arts courses, Red Cross groups, etc – all of these could improve self confidence and give an opportunity to meet new people. Local councils and libraries will be able to give you an idea of what is available.

If you feel that your child needs legal advice, contact the Children's Legal Centre.
If your child has been injured or threatened, you can contact the police. Only keep your child home if you are worried about their safety or if you feel that they are desperate.

See SECTION 4: RESOURCES for telephone numbers of national help organisations or you could include your own local agencies.

ADVICE FOR PARENTS OF CHILDREN WHO ARE BULLYING
(can be adapted for use as a Handout for Parents)

The following might be useful advice when talking with parents who are trying to help their child stop bullying behaviour:

1. Ask your child if s/he can explain what has happened and why – try not to be too judgemental at this point

2. Talk with your child and find out if there are ways you can work together to stop his/her behaviour

3. Explain that the bullying must stop and that the situation could become worse if it doesn't (the possibility that the child might be suspended from school or that police action might have to be taken in serious cases should be discussed, if appropriate)

4. Explain how frightening the bullying is for the victim and try to encourage empathy

5. Criticise the bullying behaviour, but don't reject your child or label him/her as a 'bully' ('What you did was wrong' instead of 'You are a terrible person' or 'You're a bully')

KIDSCAPE: How to stop bullying

6. Look for good behaviour from your child and praise it, even if it is something small like closing the door without slamming it or picking up clothes and putting them away

7. Tell your child you know s/he can change the bullying behaviour – say that you know the child is NOT really a bully. Give your child the confidence to try to change

8. If possible help your child to develop new interests and/or friends away from the 'bully gang'. Work on improving his/her social skills – how to approach people, how to say nice things, how not to react if s/he is angry etc (See SECTION 2: WORKING WITH BULLIES AND VICTIMS for practical ways to help change bullying behaviour)

9. Try to spend as much time with your child as you can, especially listening to his/her concerns. Sometimes children bully other children as a way of getting attention

10. Make it clear that you do not accept bullying behaviour and that there will be consequences at home such as no television or loss of privileges if the bullying does not stop

You might also decide to give parents copies of the KIDSCAPE booklets on bullying, especially 'Preventing Bullying: A Parent's Guide' and 'You Can Beat Bullying: A Guide for Young People'. These booklets can be obtained directly from KIDSCAPE.

See SECTION 4: RESOURCES for the telephone numbers of national help organisations or you could include the numbers of local agencies.

Dealing with bullying is covered in the National Curriculum in Curriculum Guidance 5: Health Education:

SAFETY

'The acquisition of knowledge and understanding of safety in different environments, together with the development of associated skills and strategies, helps pupils to maintain their personal safety and that of others.'

KEY STAGE 1

* DEVELOP AND BE ABLE TO PRACTISE SIMPLE WAYS OF KEEPING SAFE AND FINDING HELP

KEY STAGE 2

* BE ABLE TO KEEP SAFE AND USE BASIC SAFETY PROGRAMMES

* BE ABLE TO ACCEPT RESPONSIBILITY FOR SAFETY OF THEMSELVES AND OTHERS

KEY STAGE 3

* BE ABLE TO ANALYSE AND ASSESS SITUATIONS IN TERMS OF SAFETY

KEY STAGE 4

* BE ABLE TO INVESTIGATE AND DEMONSTRATE SAFE PRACTICES IN VARIOUS ENVIRONMENTS, EG HOME, SCHOOL

1 REDUCING PLAYGROUND BULLYING: *Ideas and Resources*

We hope the following list of suggestions, although not exhaustive, will stimulate your own ideas.

Playgrounds should be places where children can play and have fun in a safe and secure setting. However, they are sometimes places where children are bored, or frightened, or frustrated, and where bullying and fights happen everyday.

You don't need a great deal of money to turn the most unprepossessing asphalt area into a place which even timid children can enjoy using. We hope that these suggestions will give you some practical and inexpensive ideas which you can use to improve your own playground.

● Conduct a Survey using a Questionnaire to find out what the children think of the playground: ask them
  * what do they do in the playground?
  * what games they play?
  * what they like about the playground?
  * what they dislike about the playground?
  * do older children monopolize all the space?
  * do younger children feel vulnerable?
  * is there bullying?
  * do children fight in the playground?
  * what causes trouble?
  * what would they like to have in the playground?

● Find out what the staff and playground supervisors think of the playground:
  * is full use being made of the space?
  * is it being used as educational resource?
  * are playground conflicts spilling over into the classroom?
  * are there areas which are hidden from general view?
  * is there enough supervision?
  * what do they think could be done to improve the playground?

● Hold a Parents Meeting and make sure the PTA is fully involved in all the planning and decisions. Ask for parents' advice and suggestions. Ask them to suggest people in the local community who might be able to help. Find out if any of them have skills which could be used for improvements (eg. builders, painters).

● Talk to local contractors (builders, landscape gardeners, painters). Ask for their advice and help.

● Find out if local companies would be prepared to sponsor new equipment or contribute towards the cost of refurbishment.

● Have a working party or playground committee – give them a term to come up with a design for a new-style playground and plan of action.

● Put up a playground noticeboard for announcements, competitions, suggestions.

● Make it clear that fighting and kicking are outlawed. Involve the children in a project to decide on a series of positive rules for acceptable behaviour in the playground. Get each class to come up with five or ten points. Some of the things children have suggested include:
    * no kicking,
    * no punching or pulling hair
    * no fighting
    * asking before joining in a game
    * sharing space
    * respecting the quiet area
    * inviting left-out children to join in
    * making sure new pupils have someone to talk to

Use the children's suggestions to draw up a five or ten point Playground Code. Put it up on the playground noticeboard, and make sure every child and parent has a copy. Explain that breaking these rules will not be tolerated.

● If fighting or bullying are common, complement the positive changes to the playground by introducing a whole-school anti-bullying policy.

● Use role-plays in class to find different ways of resolving conflict. Ask the children to dramatise situations they have witnessed in the playground which resulted in bullying or fighting. What could they have done to help? Encourage them to think of alternative ways of responding to aggressive behaviour.

● Whenever possible, stagger children's playtimes so that there are not too many children in the playground at any one time. Separate the older children so that they play at a different time to younger ones.

- Install a camera overlooking the playground (it could be a dummy – many security firms supply them) or take photographs very obviously (it doesn't matter if there is no film in the camera- the idea that they are being recorded makes children think twice before bullying anyone!) Make sure all the children know that their actions are being recorded – it's amazing how quickly bullying decreases when the perpetrators realise their every move is being captured on film. Real photographs are also helpful as they do away with the "I didn't do it. It wasn't me" excuse.

- Make a 'quiet' area: cordon off a section of the playground with tubs of plants or put up trellising to support climbing plants. Install some fixed seating. Explain to the children that this area is just for sitting and talking – it is not for noisy games or for hide-and-seek.

- Turn the care of the plants in the tubs over to the children – perhaps the responsibility of one particular class. As they look after the plants over the year, they can monitor growth and try out different planting schemes.

- Paint games on the playground: a noughts and crosses board, hopscotch squares, a number snake or ladder, or a 'champ' square. (Use non-toxic paint). County ground maintenance teams often have useful templates and are experienced in marking out playgrounds. No other games should be allowed to 'encroach' on the painted areas – football games, for example, can take-over every available inch of space unless there are clear limits.

- Designate an area especially for ball games, skipping, and anything else which involves running, jumping and shouting!

- Hold a series of "playground workshops" with parents and grandparents. Get older members of the community to teach children some of the games they used to play as children, and some of the songs and rhymes they used to sing. Many of the old school games are being forgotten but children still find them just as much fun as our grandparents when they are taught how to play them. Ask the children to make up new games.

- Have skipping ropes, elastic for french skipping or jingle jangle, basketballs and footballs available.

- Fix a basketball net to a wall or install a freestanding net.

- Think about turning a corner of the playground into a garden. Classes could have their own plots or areas, or one class could be responsible for maintainence. Children could try out different varieties of seed and fertilizer. Playground gardens, even small ones, can be used very succesfully as an additional resource for the science curriculum.

- If several classes or children are involved, ask a local nursery to sponsor an annual gardening prize. Successful plants and produce could be entered in local shows.

- Use the playground improvements to increase the children's awareness of their surroundings. Making a garden and planting trees or shrubs is a way of 'greening' the environment. Contact local environmental groups and the local natural history society. Involve them in designing the playground changes.

- Install a simple weather station: rain gauge, thermometer and anenometer. Have a 'weather watch team' to record day-by-day results. Hold a competition for children to guess the total amount of rainfall from the beginning of the winter term to a date before the end of the summer term. Post up the running total on the playground noticeboard so children can keep track of how they are doing.

RESOURCES

"Can I stay in today Miss?" Improving the School Playground by Carol Ross and Amanda Ryan, Trentham Books 1990, ISBN 9-780948-080425. An excellent, practical handbook with a step-by-step guide to planning playground changes.

Bright Ideas: The Outdoor Classroom edited by Brian Keaney and Bill Lucas, Scholastic Publications Ltd. 1992,
ISBN 9-780590-530347. Full of interesting, easy and inexpensive ideas for using the playground as an educational resource. All the ideas are linked to specific areas of the curriculum. Age 5-11.

Children's Games in Street and Playground by Iona and Peter Opie, OUP 1984, ISBN 0-19-288881489-3. Provides a fascinating source for all sorts of children's games.

Using School Grounds as an Educational Resource by Kirsty Young of Learning through Landscapes Trust,1990,
ISBN 1-872865-04-6. Includes 13 case studies, a detailed action plan and a pull-out wall chart.

For detailed advice and suggestions contact:

Learning through Landscapes Trust

Third Floor, Southside Offices   Tel. 01962 846258
The Law Courts   Fax 01962 869099
Winchester
Hants. SO23 9DI

SECTION 2: WORKING WITH BULLIES AND VICTIMS – CHANGING BEHAVIOUR

INTRODUCTION

Victims and children and young people who bully* may feel worthless and begin to punish themselves. They often need help to build or re-build their confidence and to learn new ways to deal with people. There are steps they can take (with help) that can change the way they feel about themselves.

1) Decide that they are not going to be victims or bullies

2) Look at themselves to see what, if anything, has led them to be the victims or bullies in the past, including specific incidents

3) If something they have done has promoted their victimisation, they need to learn new 'non-victim' behaviours

4) They need to practise more positive ways of behaving

This Section has two purposes:

1) To help adults help victims and children and young people who bully to re-learn behaviour and build up confidence

2) To enable professionals to try out ideas before they attempt to help children

The exercises are not labelled for particular ages as most have successfully been used and adapted for students of different ages and abilities.
You may also wish to try out some of the exercises in Section 3 which are designed for general use with students, but which would benefit those more directly affected by bullying.

* Please note that whenever possible we have talked about children and young people who bully in an attempt not to label them as bullies (see LABELS: EXERCISE in this SECTION). However, in the interest of brevity, we have sometimes just referred to 'bullies'.

RECOGNISING BULLYING BEHAVIOUR: *Course Notes and Exercise*

Object: To give information about the possible reasons why a child might become a bully

Time: Lecture – 15 minutes
Group discussion – 30 minutes

The information in the Course Notes below can be used as a lecture, with Handouts, or as the basis for your own workshop. After the lecture, ask the participants to break into small groups and discuss their reactions, concerns or questions about bullies. They may came up with additional points which can be compiled in a large group discussion at the end of the individual group sessions.

INTRODUCTION: Course Notes

We have already looked at how the attitudes of the staff, the ethos of the school, and the layout of the school buildings can promote bullying. It might help now to focus on other possible causes such as the child's temperament and the influence of the child's family on his/her behaviour.

CHILD'S TEMPERAMENT

Dan Olweus, Professor of Psychology at the University of Bergen in Norway, has done a considerable amount of work with children who have exhibited bullying type behaviour. He found that children who bully can be high-spirited, active, energetic children. They may be easily bored or envious and/or insecure. For example, they may be jealous of another's academic or sporting success, or they may be jealous of a sibling/new baby. They may have a learning disability which makes them angry and frustrated (though this may have the opposite effect and make them a target for bullies rather than being a bully). They may be angry or down-trodden from abuse they themselves have suffered.

Children who bully can also be spoilt brats who are just over-indulged and used to getting their own way. Sometimes we find children with no obvious problems who just seem to enjoy bullying others.

FAMILY INFLUENCE

Dan Olweus has carried out a twenty year study of children who bully and he has identified the child rearing practices of the bully's family as very significant.

Neglected Child

If the child is neglected, or picked on, or punished excessively at home, s/he may develop a very negative self-image. The child may become frustrated, anxious and insecure. They may then start to bully others in order to gain respect and to prove that they are worthy of notice.

Aggressive Family

The family may be aggressive or quick-tempered with lots of loud arguments and shouting. As this is the child's first behaviour model, they will tend to reproduce this type of aggressive behaviour when they are with other children.

If the parents are bullies, they are likely to defend or promote aggressiveness in their children – this is especially true of some macho-type parents. In one case, a boy set another's clothes on fire but, when the father of the bully was told of the incident, he was extremely aggressive and refused to accept that what his child had done was in any way responsible – 'it's his own fault if he got set on fire'.

'Anything Goes' Family.

The child may be given a great deal of license at home and so have trouble recognising what is acceptable when s/he is with other people. They may react badly to discipline. They may be spoilt and used to being the centre of attention at home.

DO WE NEED TO KNOW WHAT MAKES BULLIES TICK?

If we are intent only on punishing the bully, we don't need to know why they have become bullies. However, if we want to help the bully change his/her behaviour, we have to try to understand why they adopted bullying strategies in the first place.

Although every child who bullies is an individual, many display certain characteristics common to all bullies. Identifying those characteristics can help us discover what has driven this particular child to bullying. Identifying some of the main reasons, including particular family pressures, which might underlie a bully's behaviour makes it easier to decide on the most appropriate and effective course of action for that individual.

OCCASIONAL AND CHRONIC BULLIES

The Occasional Bully

The Occasional Bully can display kinder aspects of his/her character, but does resort to bullying when it suits. These bullies do share some of the same traits, but are difficult to classify because the bullying behaviour is not consistent and is often precipitated by some sort of crisis or by the bully 'having a bad day'. These children and young people can also be quite charming, but often they:

* are suddenly aggressive to peers, parents, teachers and siblings
* act impulsively and regret it later
* don't learn from their mistakes
* wish to be in charge
* may be physically strong
* may be articulate
* may be manipulative
* may display other anti-social behaviours, such as throwing tantrums or yelling when things go wrong
* may, on the whole, have good self esteem
* may be spoilt rotten – parents cannot understand how their children could be bullying others because they are perfect at home where their every wish is granted

This short list highlights some salient characteristics. It is not meant to be exhaustive but it should provide a useful guide.

These are characteristics we often find in children who bully *occasionally*. Their self-esteem can be quite high and they may well be very spoilt. Spoilt children who bully need firm, clear guidelines and established consequences to actions. We also have to try and teach them to empathise with other children.

96

The Chronic Bully

Chronic bullies may have some or all of the following characteristics or backgrounds (list taken from 'Keeping Safe' by Michele Elliott, Hodder/Headline, 1994)

Chronic bullies may:

* act aggressively much of the time
* be unable to control themselves
* have a positive attitude towards violence
* feel insecure
* be disruptive
* refuse to take responsibility for their actions
* have no empathy with victims
* feel inadequate
* feel humiliated
* be bullied by parents/siblings
* become scapegoats
* have been abused
* be under pressure to succeed
* not be allowed to show feelings
* feel they are different or stupid
* have no sense of accomplishment
* have poor social skills

Again, this list is not exhaustive but it can be used as a starting point.

This is the most worrying type of bullying behaviour. These are the children who go from incident to incident, from school to school, and who may eventually end up being excluded from mainstream education. They are very often the victims of bullying at home where they are constantly told that they can't do anything right and that they are inadequate and useless. These children attack weakness in others, thus giving themselves a sense, however illusory, of power and accomplishment.

It is hard to change the behaviour of this group, especially when they are allowed to continue behaving in this way until they cause particular trouble as teenagers. Without intensive help, this kind of bully is more likely to go on to commit crimes and cause great distress to others throughout their lives.

THREE MAIN TYPES OF BULLY

Occasional and Chronic bullies are useful short-hand labels devised by KIDSCAPE, but Dan Olweus has studied bullies very closely and has identified three main types. Their chief characteristics are summarized below.

1. AGGRESSIVE BULLY (majority of bullies are in this group)

* aggressive
* poor impulse control
* positive view of violence
* wishes to dominate
* physically & emotionally strong
* insensitive to feelings of others
* good self esteem

2. ANXIOUS BULLY (about 20% of bullies – this tends to be the most disturbed group)

* anxious & aggressive
* low self esteem
* insecure & friendless
* pick on 'unsuitable' victims (ie. more powerful than them)
* provoke attacks by other bullies
* emotionally unstable

3. PASSIVE BULLY (these get involved in bullying as they become followers of the bully to protect themselves and to have the status of belonging to the dominant group.)

* easily dominated
* passive & easily led
* not particularly aggressive
* have empathy for other's feelings
* feel guilty after bullying

HURTING OTHERS

One way of identifying bullies is through the way they react when they have caused emotional or physical pain. The normal reaction is to admit the wrong immediately, even if only to oneself, and then try to make up for it. Usually people feel genuine remorse and will apologise. However, bullies have difficulty in admitting that they have done something wrong. They suppress their natural guilt and, because they do not feel remorse, have no hesitation in repeating the hurtful action.

These reactions can be contrasted as follows (adapted from 'Nasty People' by Jay Carter, Contemporary Books, Chicago, 1989):

Chronic Bully Reaction after hurting someone:
* Justify hurting them to oneself
* Suppress guilt – which often becomes bad mood
* Avoid atonement

Normal Reaction after hurting someone:
* Admit wrongdoing, at least to oneself
* Feel guilty
* Atone – do something to make up

The information in this section is summarised in the next five Overheads which can be used for group work.

Further reading:

Valerie Besag: Bullies and Victims in Schools, Open University Press, 1989.

Jay Carter: Nasty People, How to stop being hurt by them without becoming one of them, Contemporary Books, Chicago, 1989.

Michele Elliott: Keeping Safe, a Practical Guide to Talking with Children, Hodder/Headline, 1994. (available from KIDSCAPE)

Michele Elliott (ed): Bullying, A Practical Guide to Coping for Schools, Longman, 1991. (Available from KIDSCAPE)

Dan Olweus: Bullying at School: What we know and what we can do, Blackwell, 1994.

John Pearce: Fighting, Teasing and Bullying. Effective ways to help your child cope with aggressive behaviour, Thorsons, 1989.

John Pearce: What can be done about the Bully? in Bullying: A Practical Guide to Coping for Schools, ed. Michele Elliott, Longman, 1991.

2

SOME CAUSES OF BULLYING

1. Layout and Ethos of School

2. Attitude of Staff

3. Temperament of Child

* aggressive
* active
* quick tempered
* jealous

SOME CAUSES OF BULLYING (continued)

4. Influence of Family

a) negative attitude of primary caretaker

* lack of warmth
* lack of involvement
* favouring another sibling

b) power assertive child-rearing methods

* physical punishment
* violent emotional
* outbursts

c) "anything goes" family

* spoilt child
* child gets his/her own way
* no discipline or limits

THE OCCASIONAL BULLY

may display some or all of the following characteristics:

* **be aggressive to peers, parents, teachers and siblings**

* **be impulsive**

* **wish to be in charge**

* **display good self esteem – bullying makes him/her feel important**

* **be physically strong**

* **be articulate/manipulative**

* **have other anti-social behaviours**

* **be spoilt**

KIDSCAPE: How to stop bullying

CHRONIC BULLIES MAY:

* **Feel insecure**

* **Feel inadequate**

* **Feel humiliated**

* **Be bullied by parents/siblings**

* **Become scapegoats**

* **Have been abused**

* **Be under pressure to succeed**

* **Not be allowed to show feelings**

* **Feel they are different**

* **Have no sense of accomplishment**

From Keeping Safe by Michele Elliott

HURTING OTHERS

Chronic Bully Reaction after hurting someone:

* Justify hurting them to oneself

* Suppress guilt – becomes bad mood

* Avoid atonement

Normal Reaction after hurting someone:

* Admit wrongdoing, at least to oneself

* Feel guilty

* Atone-do something to make up

From Nasty People by Jay Carter

BULLY GANGS: *Course Notes*

WHY DO CHILDREN JOIN GANGS?

Gangs are most popular in adolescence when children are beginning to break away from parental control. Gangs formed in primary school tend to be much looser and less structured than those formed by teenagers.

Reasons for joining include:

* pressure to conform, to be liked and accepted

* fear of being bullied/ostracised if you don't join in

* way of protecting oneself from harm – if you're one of the gang, you can't be one of the victims

* boredom – gangs can be exciting

* you don't have to be particularly talented to join

* way of strengthening peer ties

* need for a leader – someone to admire and emulate

* gives status

Quite often members of bully gangs may themselves be victims of bullying. They may have been bullied into joining the gang and threats and intimidation may be used to keep them 'loyal' to the gang leader. They may have no wish to bully others themselves and may go along with the gang's bullying because it is the easiest option. It is certainly easier for them, especially if they are victims themselves, than standing up to the gang leader and saying that bullying is wrong.

Interviewing several members of a group involved in an incident can be fraught with problems. It is a good idea to have thought out the process before starting down the path. Otherwise the whole thing may blow up. If the incident is a serious one involving lots of people, it may take most of the day to sort out. It means that a senior, experienced member of staff has to devote a great deal of time to resolving the problem. It means that the individuals need somewhere to write or otherwise record their account of what happened – separately from each other. They certainly need to be kept apart and supervised when interviews begin. This might also cut across lunch and break times, when everyone must eat, or go to the toilet.

Since life in schools and institutions goes on, lessons and activities have to continue, visitors, meetings and telephone calls get in the way. It is not easy!

BEFORE EMBARKING ON THE PROCESS TRY TO ENSURE THAT:

*   the accounts, written or recorded are under control

*   everyone who needs supervision is settled for as long as it takes (this could be one supervisor or a series of supervisors taking turns simply looking after the individuals, perhaps in a classroom, while the main interviews are taking place elsewhere, perhaps in the Head's room

*   you are prepared to have a student with you at break, if necessary

*   you have not pre-judged the issues. Give all the parties the respect they deserve – some or all may not be guilty of anything.

BREAKING UP BULLY GANGS

*   Set in motion the usual school procedures for dealing with bullying incidents

*   Try to get an apology to the victim/s and restitution or compensation for goods or money stolen or lost

*   When interviewing bully gangs after an incident, see the gang members separately. If you see them all together, they will support each other and draw strength from their own numbers. If you see them alone, the weaker members will not be intimidated by the leader's presence and may therefore feel able to talk freely about what happened and why. See the individual members as quickly as possible after the incident so they don't have time to plan what they are all going to say. Ask each individual to write down or record in some way (perhaps with a tape recorder if writing is a problem, or by giving their account to an adult who notes it down) what happened.

*   Once you've spoken to all the gang members individually, you can then bring the gang together. Ask each member to repeat what they said in their private interview in front of everyone else. If anyone tries to change their story, you already have their written report of what happened. *This is one of the most important aspects of the whole process because you are breaking down the gang solidarity.* No one can fool someone else by saying afterwards "I didn't say anything" and trying to act big in front of the other gang members.

Each person has admitted their part and, hopefully, expressed the way s/he is going to make up for what has happened. At the end of this meeting everyone should be clear about what happened and why. No one can pretend they did not take part or that they managed to fool the staff about what happened.

* Prepare the gang to face their peer group. You need to give some thought to what the gang members are going to say when they leave the meeting. You don't want them going out saying things which will increase their status with their peers (eg. "They had to have a *special* meeting to talk to us."). Get everyone to agree what they will say about the meeting. For example, "It was about homework" (a lie, of course, which can create other problems), or agree to say "it's confidential" or "none of your business" (which could provoke a nasty response!) The important thing is that *everyone sticks to the same story.* Anyone who doesn't and who tries to use the incident to further their own status or to bully again faces further sanctions.

* Sanctions imposed on the gang might include:
    - not being allowed to have breaks or play together
    - being separately confined to different areas of the playground
    - not being allowed to sit together
    - breaking up the group into separate classes
    - eating separately

* Ask each gang member in turn how they are going to ensure that they are not involved in bullying again. Stress that those who stand around whilst other members of the gang are actively involved in bullying someone are just as much to blame. There is no such thing as the 'innocent bystander' when it comes to bullying. (See next set of COURSE NOTES for further information about BYSTANDERS.) If any one of them witnesses a bullying incident, they should either try to intervene to stop it or get help or they will be in trouble again.

* Reiterate that bullying is not acceptable. Repeat the anti-bullying provisions of the School Contract. Explain again that sanctions will be imposed on those who ignore the Contract and continue to bully other pupils.

* At the end thank everyone for their help in 'co-operating' – even if the co-operation was grudging.

* Let everyone know the outcome, including parents, and say that you expect this to be the end of it all.

* You may need to do more work with the class/year involved to reinforce the message that bullying in any form is not tolerated. Roleplays, discussions, essays, drama projects can all be used to heighten children's awareness of bullying and how they can help stop it. (See SECTION 3 for practical exercises.)

KIDSCAPE: How to stop bullying

BYSTANDERS: *Course Notes*

Some of the things we are often told after a bullying incident by those children who were not directly involved are "It wasn't me", "It's not my fault", or "I didn't do anything". They assume that, because they just stood around and took no active part in the bullying, they bear no responsibility for what happened.

Children need to learn that when bullying is involved there is no such thing as an 'innocent bystander'. If you were there, if you saw what was happening, and you did nothing to stop it then you were involved.

Children may not have intervened because they were frightened of getting hurt, or frightened of becoming the next victim, or they may just have been glad that it wasn't them this time. These responses are understandable but they are not acceptable in the context of a whole-school anti-bullying policy.

The word 'empowering' comes to mind. Both victims and onlookers (even sometimes bullies) ought to feel that they are empowered by the anti-bullying ethos and that it is safe for them to tell if they are bullied themselves or if they see someone being bullied. They can have a hand in their own destiny. They are not just victims of the bully who are forced to suffer in silence. They can tell without fear of reprisals or ridicule.

Children in any school ought to feel part of the safety regime in which they are protected, and have permission to speak out about danger (asbestos, fire), tyranny (bullies, teachers), harassment (racial, sexual, verbal), abuse, or any other issue which is affecting their lives or the lives of friends. Building this safe environment is up to the adults.

Exercises which help raise children's awareness of bullying and of the suffering of victims can be used to make the point that nobody should ignore bullying or let it go unchallenged. (See SECTION 2 and SECTION 3 for practical exercises for use with children and young people.) A whole-school policy means every single person in the school has to take responsibility for stopping bullying.

Everyone who witnesses a bullying incident has a duty either to intervene or to get help. Witnesses can help the victim by standing with them, saying No and getting the victim away, or they can get help from adults or older students. The important thing is that witnesses or bystanders should act positively to end the bullying.

Anyone who just stands and watches bullying (or any form of harm) take place, or who just walks on past, is actually allowing the bullying to continue. They are condoning what is happening. In a school or institution with a whole school anti-bullying policy ignoring bullying is wrong. If children feel they cannot intervene themselves, then they should tell and get help.

RECOGNISING VICTIMS: *Course Notes and Exercise*

Object: To help staff recognise the possible causes why a child or young person may be bullied

Time: Lecture – 15 minutes. Discussion – 30 minutes

You may use the information in the Course Notes below as a lecture or as the basis for your own Workshop. After the lecture, ask the participants to break into small groups. These groups can then discuss the issues and raise concerns or add new information to the discussion based upon their own experiences.

The information can be shared in a large group discussion with each small group making one or two points, depending upon the time you have available.

DIFFERENT TYPES OF VICTIMS: *Course Notes*

It is important to note that children can become victims of bullying for many reasons, but the real cause of bullying is the bully him/herself. Bullies need victims and they will find a reason to bully someone. Bullying is rarely the fault of the victim. Most victims are gentle, intelligent children who cannot understand why they have been singled out. The sad fact is that the bullies will carry on singling out people until they find enough victims to satisfy their need to dominate and hurt.

Research has been carried out about victims and it has been found that they do share some common characteristics. It might be useful to know what has been discovered in order to help the victims gain or regain their confidence. Dan Olweus and others have identified some different 'types' of victims:

Chronic Victims
* Passive Victims
* Active or Provocative Victims

'Different' Victims

Accidental Victims

Special Needs Victims

Victims because of:
* Race, Religion, Language, Culture or Sex

CHRONIC VICTIMS

These children always seem to end up being bullied – at home, in school, in activities, in organisations such as scouts or guides or youth groups, etc. It is difficult to tell if they feel badly about themselves because they have experienced bullying from a young age, either at home or in school so that the bullying created the 'victim' mentality, or if they had other problems which led to them being singled out for bullying.

Chronic victims often:

* feel badly about themselves and have low self esteem
* find that bullying is reassuring because it confirms their low opinion of themselves
* get upset if told they are good because it doesn't fit into their self image
* destroy their own good work
* say no one likes them
* are over-sensitive and/or intense
* lack humour
* are slow to settle into new situations
* are jumpy & wary of people

These are children who seem to be bullied wherever they go. Changing schools in order to avoid a persistent bully often has little effect because these children are quickly 'identified' as victims by their new classmates. The bullying then begins all over again in the new surroundings.

Dan Olweus divides Chronic Victims into two main types: the Passive Victim and the Active or Provocative Victim,

Passive Victims seem to:

* be anxious and insecure
* be sensitive and quiet
* react to bullying by crying and withdrawal
* have a negative self image
* feel they are failures
* lack confidence
* be lonely and isolated from peers, teachers and others, but very close to parents
* act younger than their peers and be timid
* be unlikely to retaliate

KIDSCAPE: How to stop bullying

The passive victim is usually isolated and insecure with poor social skills and low self-esteem. They may be timid, sensitive and easily frightened. When people talk about the "typical victim", they usually have this type of victim in mind. They may have been bullied for a long time before telling someone and may have come to believe much of the negative abuse hurled at them over the months/years. They react quickly and obviously to verbal abuse or physical violence by bursting into tears or blushing violently. This makes them a very satisfying target as far as the bully is concerned.

Active or Provocative Victims seem to be:

* anxious and aggressive
* provocative and 'niggly' to peers, almost as if asking to be picked on
* very disturbed in their behaviour

This type of victim has low self-esteem and a negative self-image. They may be emotionally disturbed and may actually go out of their way to provoke or attract bullying because it is one way of getting attention. Being bullied also reinforces their low self-esteem. It can be hard to change a child's opinion of him/herself when they have reached the stage of thinking "I am so awful, I deserve to be bullied." They have developed a 'victim mentality' and are locked into the role of victim.

Low Self-esteem

One thing most chronic victims of bullying have in common is low self-esteem and a negative self-image. They may have developed a negative estimate of themselves because they are always being told at home "You're hopeless/useless at this", or "You are so clumsy. Why can't you be like your sister? She never breaks anything".

Chronic victims have learned to see themselves as inadequate and as failures. They are used to being told how badly they are doing so when the bully starts to pick on them they feel reassured. After all, this is what their family tells them. When a child starts thinking like this, they are programming themselves to be victims and they may go out of their way to provoke bullies. Changing such a deeply ingrained self-image is not easy but it can be done with patience and a lot of time.

'Different' Victims

These are children who are slightly different from their fellow pupils. They may wear glasses, or a hearing aid, or have asthma, or be talented athletes, be gay or lesbian, or be academically gifted or quite good-looking – whatever the 'difference', it is enough to make them stand out from their peers.

2

KIDSCAPE: How to stop bullying

The irony is that there are millions of people with such 'differences' who are not bullied. This can be because the adults have prepared children to accommodate and value differences in people or because the children never encounter a determined bully. We have found by talking with children that subsequent bullying quite often depends upon the response of the child when first bullied. Articulate, confident children may easily deflect attempts to bully them and the bully will go off to seek easier targets. However, less confident children may well be intimidated and if the bullying persists, may eventually display some of the characteristics like low self-esteem, timidity and loneliness associated with chronic victims.

Accidental Victims

These are victims who have not been singled out particularly by the bully but who happen to be in the wrong place at the wrong time. They may become drawn into a bullying incident in which another child is the primary target, or they may be trapped by a bully or a gang of bullies just looking for someone to pick on. The majority of the victims of bullying who contact KIDSCAPE seem to fall into this category.

Special Needs Victims

These are children who have an obvious physical or mental disability. They may look and act differently from other children or have learning difficulties which make them stand out in an academic setting. These children are bullied because they are 'different'. They make an easy target for bullies, if teachers and other adults have not taught children to accept that people are people regardless of their special educational needs. For example, if a child with profound hearing loss comes into the classroom, children may react by bullying because of ignorance, when they might have reacted with understanding had they been prepared.

Children may also be bullied because of disabilities within their family, or because of a bereavement or divorce. A fully sighted girl was bullied mercilessly because both her parents were blind. Sometimes children are bullied because their parents are divorced, or because a parent has died. ("You don't have a real family. You haven't got a Dad."). In one case, a seven year old girl was constantly tormented in the playground because her father was dying of cancer and had been moved to a local hospice.

In these cases bullying can be the final straw for children who are already coping with difficult personal problems. Children can be very cruel and it is important that this sort of bullying is nipped in the bud. The victim needs to be protected from further persecution and the bullies must learn to respect other people.

Victims because of Race, Religion, Language, Culture or Sex

Children from different racial or cultural backgrounds may stand out in the crowd and so form easy targets for bullies. If English is not their first language, they may have difficulty in understanding everything that is said to them and may become the butt of cruel jokes.

Children should be taught that differences are not divisive but should be celebrated. The contribution made by people from different cultural, racial and religious backgrounds should be recognised and the exploration and acceptance of different ideas and beliefs should be encouraged. Racial and cultural bullying is typically a product of ignorance and fear and should be challenged whenever and wherever it appears.

Some children are also bullied in a sexual way – taunted because they are developing physically or accused of being 'sluts' or by having sexual comments written about them on walls or classroom boards. Often this is because of jealousy, but that doesn't help the victims.

Four Overheads are given which summarize the main points in the foregoing Notes. They can be used for groupwork.

2

VICTIMS

1. PASSIVE TYPE

**anxious & insecure
sensitive & quiet**

**reacts to bullying by crying &
withdrawal**

**negative self image; feeling of
failure; lack of confidence**

**lonely & isolated but close to
parents**

younger & weaker; timid

unlikely to retaliate

2

VICTIMS

2. ACTIVE TYPE

anxious & aggressive

provocative

disturbed

2

CHRONIC VICTIMS

* feel badly about themselves

* find bullying reassuring

* get upset if told they are good

* destroy own good work

* say no one likes them

* are oversensitive

* lack humour

* are slow to settle in

* are jumpy & wary

HELPING VICTIMS

* teach them to cope with teasing

* encourage them to talk

* make a list of what to say

* act out (roleplay) ways to cope

* shout "NO" at a mirror

* practise walking & standing confidently – check in a mirror

* draw or write about feelings

* eliminate obvious causes of bullying (smell, runny nose)

2

KIDSCAPE: How to stop bullying

HELPING VICTIMS: *Course Notes*

2

REASSURANCE AND PROTECTION

First of all, victims need reassurance. *They need to know that once they have told about being bullied, they will be protected from any further bullying.* It is up to the adults involved to ensure that bullies are not given an opportunity to exact their revenge on a victim who has plucked up courage to tell. One girl who had been bullied persistently for months finally told about her ordeal. The next day she was too frightened of what the bullies would do to her to come back to school. She telephoned the Headteacher to explain her fears. Far from reassuring her or promising that she would be safe, he remarked, "Getting hurt is the risk you take when you tell".

Members of staff should take responsibility for ensuring as best they can that victims do not suffer at the hands of bullies after they have told about bullying incidents.

It is difficult to promise 100% safety – bullies can pounce on victims away from school or in an isolated place. However, adults can:

* advise the victim about avoiding potential trouble spots
* keep the bully under fairly constant supervision
* keep the bully behind when dismissing school to allow the victim to get home safely
* arrange for a place at school where the victim can always go to if s/he feels unsafe or intimidated
* arrange for the victim to have certain members of staff s/he can find to help
* tell the victim that 'if the bully strikes again, tell us. If you don't we can't continue to help.'

HOW CAN WE HELP VICTIMS?

Since it can never be guaranteed that the bully will not try again, we have to do the best we can to set safe-guards for the victims. We also need to work with the victims to try to give them the confidence they need. Quite often adults just sit back and let kids 'get on with it'.

Victims of bullying are sometimes told to "Fight back", "Learn to stand up for yourself", "Only cowards run away", or "Don't come whingeing to me. You've got to learn to sort things like this out yourself". There are still schools, organisations and families which adhere to this 'bash'em back' mentality.

However, advocating that children fight back means that you end up with two aggressive children on your hands rather than just the original bully. Sometimes, if victims do pluck up the courage to 'fight back', they end up in trouble for provoking the fighting. If the bully is much bigger or stronger than the victim, the victim could get seriously hurt if s/he tried to fight the bully, especially if the bully is backed by a gang.

If a child tells about bullying, it is because they need help. If they could have sorted out the bullying by themselves, they would have done so. It is because they cannot 'fight back', that they need adult support to end the bullying. Telling a bullied child to sort it out themselves is just condemning them to more of the same. It is a cop-out on the part of the adults who should be protecting and supporting the child.

Having said that, some adults who were bullied as children say that the only way they stopped the bullying in the end was to bash the bully. So, while it cannot be denied that this method might work, we still advocate that fighting back is usually neither the most effective nor most positive way forward. If a victim is set on fighting back, try to ensure that s/he knows the possible consequences and that the parents of the victim take this on board. It may be that it is a parent who is pushing this method. This puts extra pressure on the victim who may need the school's support to resist the parental pressure. If you say that the school rejects this method, it may help the victim. It might be a good idea to discuss your strategies as a staff before the situation arises.

ANONYMOUS VICTIMS

One issue of controversy in helping victims is that of anonymity. On one hand, victims might not come forward if they cannot remain anonymous; on the other hand is it fair to suspect, accuse or impose sanctions on an alleged bully without the bully knowing the name of his/her accuser. The accusation could be malicious or mischievious, or the victim might have misinterpreted a situation or accused the wrong person. If at all possible, victims should be encouraged to stand up and tell. However, this can only happen if the victims feel safe, not an easy thing to guarantee. In one school the practice is to allow victims initially to remain anonymous, but to drop the anonymity when the accusations are being investigated and dealt with. This takes a great deal of tact and skill by the staff, but is working quite well. Bullying, like other kinds of abuse, does thrive on secrecy and fear. If the bullies feel that they can intimidate victims into a shamed silence, the bullying will continue unabated. Offer the victim:

* a place of safety in the school or institution
* initial constant supervision
* an older student helper or 'pilot' who can help the victim to feel more confident and protected

KIDSCAPE: How to stop bullying

Of course, if the bully is very violent, then it may be unreasonable to expect the victim to drop the cloak of anonymity without putting the victim in real danger. In cases like this, the bully may need to be excluded for the safety of other children and then given intensive counselling.

POSITIVE WAYS TO HELP VICTIMS

RECOGNISING VICTIMS earlier in this SECTION identified different types of victims.

In the case of Chronic Victims, those children and young people who have developed a victim mode of dealing with life, we have to work with the individuals to try to help them modify their expectations and, in some cases, their behaviour. Otherwise they could go through life with a victim mentality.

The following lists some of the basic steps which can be taken to help victims:

* encourage them to talk about their feelings
* eliminate obvious causes of bullying (smell, runny nose)
* build up low self-esteem (see Assertive Exercises)
* teach them to cope with teasing
* help them make a list of what to say
* act out (roleplay) ways to cope
* practise shouting "NO" really confidently – use a mirror
* practise walking & standing confidently – check in a mirror
* have them draw or write about feelings in order to help eliminate tension
* ask them to keep a diary of progress – 'Today I walked past the bully without even looking at her'; 'What the bully said didn't matter';'Told the teacher and got help'

Note: When the bully takes possessions or money, encourage children to state: 'That is mine, give it back, please'. (See ASSERTIVENESS TRAINING EXERCISES later in this SECTION.)

If the bully does not return the property, the victim should go and report it as a theft to the appropriate person in the school or institution. It should then be treated as a theft so that the bully will learn that taking things is not allowed. In a study of young offenders in detention centres, KIDSCAPE found that all were involved in unchecked bullying (most as bullies, a few as victims) at school. One lad said: 'I used to take dinner money, sweets, trainers, but no one ever grassed and I got away with it. Maybe I wouldn't have started taking cars if someone had stopped me back then.'

From the victim's point of view, telling is better than getting into a brawl about the chocolate bar, pencil, clothes or whatever, because a fight gives the bully a chance to say that the victim 'started' it by lashing out, just when the bully was 'going to give it back anyway!'

In the case of Different, Special Needs and Racial or Cultural Victims, we need to work with all the children in the school and teach them to respect other individuals, even when those individuals differ in some way from the majority.

* Explain to all the children that everyone is different, but some differences are more obvious than others, such as a physical disability like being in a wheel chair or wearing a hearing aid. Check with your local council or organisations like the Royal Society for the Blind, to see if there are any projects that can help children learn about the special needs of others. There are books, plays and shows using large child-like models which can be used to help children understand. The object is not for students to 'adopt' children with special educational needs, or to use them like a mascot or pet, but to remove the possiblity of ridicule or fear so that all children have the chance to be included and not bullied. (See SECTION 3).

* With issues of race, culture or language differences, ensure that the children learn about the positive aspects of different cultures. Again, there are organisations within the local councils and materials available to help with this. (See SECTION 3).

Sexual harrassment is another area which should be brought into the open. Because children will be bullied with sexual comments .and/or teased about being gay, it is vital to tell all the children that these kind of comments will not be tolerated and that this kind of bullying should be reported and will be severely dealt with. Writing or saying things like 'slut' or 'homo' can be particularly devastating to a child. Most children feel unsure or confused about sexuality so the issue of bullying with sexual connotations could be part of the sex education programme, as well as a bullying issue. The Health Education Authority and other organisations have materials which might be helpful. (See SECTION 1: GAY AND LESBIAN BULLYING.)

(SECTION 3 includes practical Exercises which can be used with children and young people to bring some of the issues which can lead to bullying out into the open for discussion.)

When setting up your whole school policy (see SECTION 1) or putting together a contract (see SCHOOL CONTRACTS in SECTION 1), ensure that all of these issues are included. If it is clear to the children from the beginning that bullying in any circumstances using any of the above issues is not on, then you will eliminate some problems from the start.

ENCOURAGE THE VICTIMISED CHILD TO TALK

Many children who are victims of bullying feel very isolated and lonely. Taking the time to sit and talk to them can be very rewarding for the child. If their self-esteem is low, the very fact that a member of staff is actually bothering with them can help boost their morale. Finding the time is not easy and some would say impossible, but it pays dividends for the child. It may be that the child will need more extensive help than you can give and you will need to refer that child and parents to child guidance, educational psychologist or other suitable counsellor but, in the meantime:

* *Listen* to what they have to say about the bullying and about why they think they are being bullied. If the child has unpleasant personal habits or is dirty or smelly, talk about this and explain to the child what he/she can do to remedy the situation.

* *Praise* them for having the courage to tell about the bullying.

* *Reassure* them that the bullying will stop and steps will be taken to ensure that it is not repeated.

* Explain that you want to *help them feel better about themselves*. If possible, ask a member of staff to be available to listen to them, whenever possible.

Build up Low Self-Esteem

Helping to build up low self-esteem can take a long time (six months and upwards) but giving the child a new, positive image of him/herself can revolutionize their life.

Children with low self-esteem have to learn that they have good qualities as well as the 'bad' qualities which they are used to focusing on to the exclusion of anything that could be considered 'good'. You have to help them create a different picture of themselves, a picture of someone with talent and ability. This is revolutionary for the child and you will need patience to persist in the face of what can sometimes seem like the child's determination to hang on to their negative self-image.

* identify a subject or activity the child is good at or particularly enjoys – praise them for their effort and achievement. Talk to the member of staff who takes the child for this subject/activity. Explain what you are doing and enlist their co-operation. Give the child opportunities to shine and lots of praise and encouragement.

* give the child some extra responsibility – nothing too difficult as this might cause them to worry that they will not be able to cope.

KIDSCAPE: How to stop bullying

PRIMARY:

* appoint the child classroom monitor – tidying desks and handing out books etc.

* assign them as 'pilots' for new pupils – they can look after them, show them around and explain how things work

* help younger children with reading

* as a class project, have all the children bring in or draw a picture of themselves. Mount the pictures on a piece of paper (See SECTION 3 CORNUCOPIA)

Ask the parents to send in one sentence praising something their child does well, such as 'John is a brilliant swimmer'.

Have each child write something nice about every child in the class, such as 'John helped me with my maths', or 'John never does anything mean'. Put these comments under/around the pictures and put the pictures up in the classroom. Add your own comment and perhaps get other staff members to do the same. Then ask all the children to go around reading the comments to themselves.
(This idea is used in Norway and is extremely sucessful)

Ensure that the pictures are up for any parent's evening, as well. Show the comments to visitors and invite the Head in to look at the pictures and to compliment the children. Engineer it so that the victim has nice things said about him/her, but don't overdue it just for the victim. If everyone is involved, the victims won't feel singled out.

* use class meetings or Circle Time (again used in Norwegian Schools – class sits in a circle and each person is given a chance to talk without fear of ridicule or retaliation – this is described in the KIDSCAPE Primary Child Protection Programme) to help children start feeling more confident.

SECONDARY:

* assign them as 'pilots' for new pupils – as above

* help juniors with work

* use books such as 'Kes' to celebrate the individuality of children. The boy in this book is a loner and potential bully victim. His ability to communicate with kestrels – his one and only skill – brings him alive in the classroom and earns him respect. Eric Jones tells about a child who was diabetic and, in secondary school, had all the potential to be ostracised and bullied. Eric persuaded him to explain his physical condition to the class and to demonstrate injecting himself with medication. Under careful and compassionate guidance, the child's self-esteem grew as did his status with the group. The fear of the unknown was effectively dealt with, as well.

* arrange things like gym or art exhibitions, if a child has a talent you would like to encourage which might help his/her self-esteem. If it is a class or school-wide exhibition, all the better.

* encourage victims to think of things they do well or help them to develop an interest which might put them into contact with other supportive people. This could be taking a martial arts course (not to turn themselves into 'Rambo', but to foster self-confidence), or signing up for swimming, running, tennis or another sport which doesn't require a lot of participants.

Team sports are great, but may be quite daunting for a child who is being bullied. Duncan Goodhew, the Olympic Gold Metalist, was bullied because he was dyslexic and then because he lost his hair as a teenager to alopecia. He turned adversity into triumph by excelling in his individual field of swimming. Sir John Harvey Jones, also bullied at school, became a wealthy leading industrialist. Phil Collins and other famous stars apparently suffered bullying as well to varying degrees, yet they all managed to reach the top of their professions. Using role models like this can encourage victims of bullying and show them that it is possible to rise above these awful experiences.

Whatever you do with children or young people, it is important to maintain a sense of proportion – you don't want the child turning into 'teacher's pet' and being subjected to renewed bullying because they are seen to be getting too much additional attention.

KIDSCAPE: How to stop bullying

COPING WITH TEASING

Teasing can be very hurtful (see DEFINITION OF BULLYING in SECTION 1) and some children, especially only children, can find teasing at school devastating.

When listening to children telling us that they have been hurt by teasing, it can sometimes be tempting to dismiss the child's complaint by saying "It's just words – they can't hurt you." Words do hurt and, whatever we as adults may feel, the important thing is that the child is deeply upset by what has been going on.

Victims don't know how to react to teasing; they don't know how to laugh at themselves or how to shrug off comments. One way of helping children cope with teasing is by teaching them low-key ways of reacting. The key is to deflect the teasing without encouraging the bully. You can help victims by working out different responses they could make to insults and teasing.

For example, if a child wears glasses and is taunted by being called 'Four-eyes', a quick response might be "Four eyes are better than two". A snappy retort like this will often disconcert a bully, especially if the child has previously responded by blushing or crying. The responses don't have to be very clever or complicated. The important thing is to encourage the victim to say something confidently back to the bully. A response like 'Thank you' works wonders – what can you say when someone just keeps saying 'Thank you'?

Work out several different responses the child could make. Another way of responding is to provide a straightforward aknowledgement: "Yes, I wear glasses. I am shortsighted." This doesn't give the bully much satisfaction. Another response might be "Yes, I wear glasses. So what?"

Victims should try not to show they are upset – bullies soon get tired of victims who never reveal their emotions. As well as practising different verbal responses to taunts, victims should also practice walking away from the bully, taking deep breaths to calm themselves down, or going to a 'time-out' room. It is very hard for a bully to continue bullying someone who is either apparently unaffected or who just walks away.

ACT OUT WAYS OF COPING

When you have come up with some different ways of coping with the bullying, roleplay them with the victim. Ask the victim's parents to help with this. Get them to practise the different responses with the victim at home. The victim has to be encouraged to use the new strategies and the more practice they have, the more confident they will feel.

PRACTISE SAYING NO AND WALKING CONFIDENTLY

The victim should practise shouting 'NO' really loudly and confidently in front of a mirror. It can really put a bully off if the formerly meek and submissive victim turns and bellows 'NO'. The victim should then walk away, quickly and without looking back. Don't hang about waiting for a confrontation!

The victim can also practise walking 'tall'. The victim's body language can often reflect they way they feel about themselves. They may stoop, hang their heads, and hunch themselves into as small a space as possible. Practise standing up straight, holding the head high, and taking deep breaths. This is a good exercise to do with victims at the beginning of assertiveness training sessions. Stand 'like victims' and then stand 'like heroes'.

DRAW OR WRITE ABOUT FEELINGS

Victims should be encouraged to express their feelings about the bullying and about themselves through painting, essays and poems. Such activities give victims an opportunity to 'get their feelings out' and bring out their concerns. They also enable children to keep a safe distance from frightening events and emotions and gives them a chance to work on ways of dealing with them.

Bottling up the feelings leads to illness, depression and sometimes to suicide attempts, some of which unfortunately succeed.

KEEP A DIARY OF PROGRESS

It can be very helpful for the victim to keep a diary of their achievements and successes which you can review with them every week. This diary should also mention times when the victim found it hard to remember or carry out the new strategies and should contain resolutions about future behaviour.

If the victim is having difficulties, explain that everyone finds learning new ways of behaving difficult and that you are very proud of the victim for all their hard work so far.

HELPING VICTIMS: *Exercise*

Object: To apply some of the ways of helping victims discussed in the HELPING VICTIMS COURSE NOTES to individual cases

Time: 15-30 minutes

Ask participants to divide into groups. Give each group a copy of the CASE STUDIES OF VICTIMS HANDOUT which follows this Exercise. Ask each group to choose one case to discuss. It doesn't matter if more than one group looks at one of the cases. Ask each group to come up with five points of action.

Then ask each group to feed back one or two points of action.

2

CASE STUDIES OF VICTIMS

JENNY

Jenny has never been a problem, but lately she is unhappy, silent and avoids the other children on the playground. She has started staying away from classes. She cries, but won't say what is the matter. You have no evidence of bullying, but you suspect that this is the root of the problem.

MARINA

Marina tearfully reports that she is being called 'nig nog, monkey, smelly, kinky hair' and other names by the children in her class. One boy, in particular, taunts her when no one else is around. You don't know if he has ever racially harassed anyone before or why this class has suddenly adopted racist abuse. There hasn't been a problem with racist bullying in that year before.

TONY

Tony has been a victim of bullying in his previous school. He recently joined your school and the bullying seems to be starting again. You are puzzled because the children bullying him have not caused any problems in the past. Tony looks miserable most of the time, but you also note that he seems to invite bullying by behaving inappropriately (suddenly becoming silly, telling dumb jokes, barging into activities) so that the other children are frustrated by his actions. Tony's parents are upset that it is 'starting all over again'. They expect you to stop it.

SAHID

Sahid arrives at school, bruised, bleeding and with torn clothing. He says he fell down, but you know that isn't the case. This has happened in the past. Then another gang of older kids from another school beat him. The police were called and it stopped, or so you thought. Sahid is clearly terrified to tell you who did it and you are equally determined that this is serious and should be dealt with immediately. You suspect that threats were used to keep the boy quiet. (You can change this scenario by having the bullies come from your own school – would you handle the situation differently?).

CASE STUDIES OF VICTIMS, continued.

JANE

Jane is in year 8. Her mother is a lesbian and has lived with her partner since Jane was at Nursery School. Jane is very unhappy because a group in her year taunt her all the time, saying she must be a lesbian like her mother. They have nicknamed her 'Jane the dyke'. Jane has come to see you because she has just found graffitti about herself in the lavatories. She is pale and shaking.

FAHIM

Fahim wears glasses, always completes homework on time and gets good grades. However, over the last few weeks his work has become very slapdash. Other Asian boys in Fahim's year used to play football in the playground and join in whatever was going on but the playground supervisors say that now these Asian students are very subdued, huddling in groups and talking but not playing games. This morning Fahim has a black eye and his glasses are taped together. He is obviously very upset but all he will say is that he fell on his way home.

You think Fahim has been beaten up and you suspect that the other Asians in his year are being bullied or harassed in some way but you don't know if it's happening in school or outside.

SARAH

Sarah is at a girl's boarding school. She is normally very cheerful but over the past week she has begun to look pale and ill. When you ask her if anything is the matter, she bursts into tears and says that no one in her class has spoken to her for a week. She has been 'sent to Coventry'. The other girls say she can't join their conversations because she doesn't have a boyfriend and won't be able to 'understand' what they are talking about. They also say that she is so fat no one will ever find her attractive. By now Sarah is sobbing and you take her to the School Nurse who puts her to bed in the sick bay.

2

KIDSCAPE: How to stop bullying

CHANGING THE BULLY'S BEHAVIOUR: *Course Notes*

Once you have dealt with the immediate fall-out from the latest bullying incident, you are ready to begin on the longterm task of helping the child who bullies to change so that s/he develops other non-bullying ways of behaving and reacting. This is a lengthy, time-consuming process with no guarantees of success but it is an essential part of an effective whole-school anti-bullying policy.

It must be emphasised that getting the the child who bullies to change his/her behaviour works best in the context of a clearly formulated whole school policy in which the children feel they have a say. Peer pressure is one of the most effective ways of stamping out bullying but children and young people will only outlaw bullying amongst themselves after they have decided that bullying is loser behaviour and that it is safe to stand up against bullying. This kind of attitude may come about through discussions, roleplays, drawing up and signing contracts, and understanding what is and what is not acceptable behaviour between individuals and groups. Or you may be lucky and have a group of children or young people who have strong, positive leaders who refuse to allow bullying to take place. (If you do, please let us know so we can all come to your school!)

There are no definitive solutions or strategies for changing a bully's behaviour which *always* work. Each child who bullies is an individual with his/her own problems and there is no general 'cure' for bullying. However guide-lines as to what has worked with bullies elsewhere can be helpful.

Some possible strategies are discussed here. This is not meant to be an exhaustive list – you may have other strategies which work wonders. However, this list may make a useful starting point when devising effective ways of deal with bullying behaviour.

Expectations

Discuss with the child or young person the behaviour which is expected of them. Take them through the School Contract again. Give them clear guidelines as to the their future behaviour. This will help to eliminate any future misunderstandings.

Admit wrong

Before you can begin to change the child's behaviour, the child has to *admit* that what they have done is wrong. They need to acknowledge in some way that their behaviour has been hurtful and unkind. This might be very difficult for some children or young people to do, but it is important that we teach children that taking responsibility for their actions is a positive way forward. If the bully is not mature enough to do this, then one way to begin to help him/her is to change the focus slightly by saying:

'Let's not talk about you for the moment. Let's say that someone else did this (describe similar bullying scenerio, but remove it from the school/institution) and the victim was someone you liked. Let's say you saw this happen – what would you do? How would you feel?' The questions obviously depend upon the ability of the bully to empathise with anyone, but it is a less threatening way to get the bully to start thinking about his/her actions.

Apologising

Children and young people who bully need to begin to realise that it is important to *apologise* to the victim and to try to *make up* in some way for what they have done. It may not happen at first. Keep trying and even roleplay with bullies because they may not know how to apologise if their family does not use or value such behaviour.

The child or young person may apologise, however grudgingly, and hand back stolen items or money, without feeling any remorse, only anger that they have been 'found out'. This does not mean the apology is meaningless. It is merely a starting point and is one way of bringing home to the bully that what they have done is unacceptable.

Short-term goals

Discuss the next steps with the child or young person and set him/her realistic short-term goals. Make sure that these goals are attainable, even if you set something like 'No fighting or saying anything mean for the next ten minutes'. It is better to give the person an easy target, even if you think it ludicrously simple, thus virtually guaranteeing their success, rather than set them a hard task which they might fail and which might discourage them.

Some of the strategies and exercises which you can use to help change bullying behaviour are set out in detail later in this SECTION. Exercises for victims and bullies have been included in the same section as the dividing line between bully and victim can be very fine. Often they share the same problems: low self-esteem, lack of social skills, etc.

ISOLATED INCIDENT –
DON'T MAKE A MOUNTAIN OUT OF A MOLEHILL

* If this is the first time that the child has been involved in a bullying incident, there may be a particular reason why the child behaved in this way at this time. The child may be under stress because:

- of work or exam pressure
- a problem that's cropped up at home (bereavement, parents separating)
- a quarrel with a friend – they might vent their anger on someone else
- boredom
- frustration – learning or language difficulties

Any of these difficulties might trigger bullying behaviour in a child who normally behaves well with other children.

* Discussion of the problem with the child will help – they may just need to talk over their problem with someone.

* Reiterate that bullying is not acceptable in any circumstances and that it will not be tolerated in the school.

* Give the child a short-term goal: 'Don't repeat the offence (fighting, kicking, stealing, etc) this morning.'

* Gradually extend the time period for good behaviour: 'Don't repeat the offence today, tomorrow/this week.'

* Work out some alternative ways the child could react if the situation occurs again. Make it something concrete that the child can do like:

- going to a 'time-out room' in which to cool off
- walking away
- deep breathing – relaxation exercises
- counting to ten

* Give the child plenty of praise and encouragement if they don't repeat the offence and are able to use some of the alternative responses.

* If the child is coping with a crisis like a parental divorce or the death of someone close to them, s/he may need emotional support, ie. someone to talk to or professional counselling.

KIDSCAPE: How to stop bullying

CHRONIC BULLYING

* If the child is often involved in bully incidents, find out if there is a pattern to the bullying. (This is one reason why it is helpful to keep reports of every bullying incident.)

● How long has the bullying been going on?
● Do particular situations provoke the bully?
● Is there just one victim or does the bully target several children?

The answers to these questions will help you identify what triggers bullying in this particular child.

You also need to consider the temperment of the child (see RECOGNISING BULLIES in this SECTION)

* Draw up some clear behaviour guidelines on how you expect the child to behave in future. If the person has never been taught acceptable ways of behaving at home, they may need some very basic information about generally accepted standards of behaviour.

* If the child has very low self-esteem, as is very often the case, you need to work on improving their self-image (see this SECTION: EXERCISES WITH BULLIES AND VICTIMS). Give them extra responsibilities. Increase responsibility gradually otherwise the child might panic because they feel they can't cope. Give them plenty of praise and encouragement when they behave well or complete tasks successfully. Help them build up their self-respect. They won't learn to respect others until they have learned to respect themselves.

* If the child is active, boisterous, quick-tempered, you need to divert their excess energy into useful activities. Get them to help with physical tasks:

● fetching and carrying jobs
● stacking books
● tidying rooms
● getting gym and games equipment ready
● putting out chairs

This way you get help and, hopefully, the child is so busy, they have no time to bully! Beware of giving them sedentary tasks – it may frustrate them and might make them twice as unruly afterwards.

* If the child is aggressive and often involved in fights, set him/her a short term goal such as 'No fighting this morning'. If they get through the morning without fighting, praise them and give them a reward – five minutes extra at break, perhaps. Get them to keep a diary of their progress. Keep reminding them of the goal.

* Gradually extend the time period ('No fighting today, tomorrow, this week) as the child learns to control his/her actions and learns different ways of reacting to difficult situations.

* Be prepared for set-backs and for discouragement. Keeping the child motivated is often very difficult and you will need all your reserves of patience and persistence!

* Discuss with the child what sort of situations make him/her flare up and then help them find other ways of reacting. Make up some simple roleplays based on what the child has told you. Have the child play him/herself and 'freeze' the action at the point where the child usually lashes out or starts challenging others – help them think about other ways of behaving: walking away, deep breathing, going to a 'time-out room' to cool off.

* Teach the child the difference between aggressive and assertive behaviour (see ASSERTIVENESS TRAINING in this SECTION). Work out verbal responses which are assertive rather than aggressive.

* Encourage the child to persist with the 'behaviour changing' programme by giving lots of praise and rewards for good behaviour.

* If the child is a bully because they are 'spoilt' at home, you may not be able to effect any fundamental behaviour changes. If aggressive behaviour is condoned in the child's home, but not allowed at school, the child is getting very mixed messages about what is and what is not allowed. Make it clear to the child that bullying behaviour will not be tolerated in the school, no matter what goes on outside. Make sure the parents know the provisions of the School Contract, and make sure they understand the consequences which face children who persist in bullying. Enforce the School Contract, impose sanctions if necessary and make it clear to the child that there are no exceptions to the no-bullying rule.

* Some children who bully have no idea of the pain and suffering their actions cause their victims. If you can find the time (and that is a big IF) try using roleplays to give bullies a chance to empathise with victims. Get the bullying child to play the victim and ask them to discuss how they feel in this unaccustomed role. One of the young offenders who took part in the KIDSCAPE Young Offender Survey had been a bully at school and he told us that he had never realised what victims of bullying suffered until he was bullied in prison. He said that he now had much more sympathy for victims and tried to stop bullying if he saw it happening.

Children who use bullying behaviour are more likely to understand how victims feel if the school has implemented an awareness-raising campaign as part of its whole school policy. (see SECTION 3).

In the KIDSCAPE Primary Schools Programme and in Teenscape there are scripted roleplays which can be used to help with this process. SECTION 3 also includes roleplays.

* If the child is frustrated and angry because of learning difficulties, remedial tuition or extra coaching may help.

* If the child is suffering through a divorce or bereavement, they may need emotional support and professional counselling.

* The child may need increased supervision. Consider assigning a teacher or another staff member to be available for the child. This could be a pastoral member of staff, or someone the child particularly likes (or who likes the child!). This person will act as a safety-valve for the child – someone they can talk to if they feel a bullying incident 'coming on'. This will be difficult with staff overburdened by work and time pressures, but it can be extremely helpful for the bullying child to have a friend they can approach for support and could save time in picking up the pieces of incidents created by bullying.

* Make sure all members of staff including playground supervisors, catering staff, and bus escort know that the child is trying to change his/her behaviour. Ask them to keep an eye on the child and to be aware of their activities. They should be ready to step in if the child becomes embroiled in difficult or hostile situations.

* It can work very well to have a child 'on report'. S/he can be reporting hourly, after every lesson, at each break, once a day or even at the end of the week. Students have a short report form which has a place for a brief comment from each teacher and a place for that teacher's signature. This works for children missing homework or who are having temporary difficulties, but it does lose its effectiveness if it goes on for too long.

KIDSCAPE: How to stop bullying

A good report should have reward of some sort – compliments, a certificate, being allowed to go on a journey that the bully might not have been going on, a letter home to parents or extra time doing something the child especially likes (not bullying!). A bad report would draw sanctions such as missing the school journey or staying in detention. We have found that not allowing children who bully their 'play' time only increases their frustration. Many of the children desperately need physical activity to let off steam, so think twice before making them stay in during recess.

* Sometimes, if children know that a child who has been a bully is trying to reform, they will try to provoke them into displaying their old, aggressive behaviour and will tease and taunt them until s/he loses control and reacts angrily. Staff should be on the look out for this sort of bully-baiting. They should also beware of making comments like "Look out, here comes trouble". This sort of remark indicates to those around the child, and to the child, that aggressive, bullying behaviour is expected of them and seems to exclude the possibility that they might behave in any other way.

* One of the best ways of helping children who bully to change their behaviour is by setting an example of the right way to behave towards other people. If bullying children see members of staff shouting at pupils, using sarcasm as a weapon, and picking on particular individuals, they will assume that, whatever anybody *says* to them, bullying is acceptable and they will have no reason to change their behaviour.

* If the child is acting in a way that could result in police being involved, someone needs to point out to the bully that s/he may be commiting a crime. We cannot duck this issue (see SECTION 1: DOES BULLYING MATTER? which looks at the some of the longterm consequences of school bullying), nor the fact that there are some incidents which we cannot deal with, especially if they involve assault or grievous bodily harm. In fact, some parents will take the issue out of our hands by pressing charges and in some cases this is the best course of action. The child needs to know this.

Do not expect instant results. It can take anything from six months to two years to change the behaviour of a child who persistently bullies others and there are likely to be many setbacks along the way. The older the child, the harder it is to change ingrained behaviour patterns, and there will always be some children whose behaviour never changes in spite of the efforts of those around them.

The following Overhead can be used for groupwork and for discussion.

CHANGING BULLY'S BEHAVIOUR

ADMIT, ACKNOWLEDGE APOLOGISE, ATONE

* **EXPLAIN WHAT IS EXPECTED OF BULLY**

* **DISCUSS & SET SHORT TERM GOALS**
  Put them in writing & get the bully (& their family if they are involved) to sign

* **REWARD ACHIEVEMENT/ GOOD BEHAVIOUR**

* **PRAISE**

* **ROLEPLAY/EMPATHY WITH VICTIM**

* **PRACTISE STRESS CONTROL, RELAXATION, WALKING AWAY**

2

CHANGING THE BULLY'S BEHAVIOUR: *Exercise 1*

Object: This Exercise gives participants an opportunity to focus on some specific bullying incidents and to work out some effective general guidelines for tackling incidents

Time: 30 minutes

Ask participants to divide into groups. Give them HANDOUT: CASE STUDIES OF BULLIES. Ask them to choose one of the three incidents and get them to come up with five different responses to each incident.

Ask each group to explain why they chose that particular incident and to report on one of the possible responses they came up with.
Are particular steps common to all responses?

OR

Ask participants to invent their own brief scenarios. They can base them on situations in their own schools. Ask them to come up with five appropriate solutions.

OR

You can also give each group the HANDOUT: I WAS THE SCHOOL BULLY. This gives some information about why this woman was a bully as a child. She never thought of herself as a 'bully'. What would participants have done to help her if they had been one of her teachers?

(You can also do this Exercise with children. Divide a class into small groups and ask each group to invent a bullying incident which could happen in the school. Ask them to say what they would do. Who would they tell? What would they say?.

This Exercise helps children focus on what exactly constitutes bullying and it also gives them an opportunity to think about ways in which they themselves can respond to incidents.)

CASE STUDIES OF BULLIES

JOHN

John has been reported for shoving a younger, weaker student against the wall in the school toilets. The victim says that he has given John money everyday for the last three weeks so that John would not 'hit him'. John has been involved in three previous incidents of bullying. He is doing poor work in school. He is not registered with the Social Services. His parents only come to school to attack the way you handle their son.

John is the leader of a gang of children who bully mainly because they are afraid that John will bully them if they do not support him. John seems to be very good at bullying, but not good at anything else. The only school activity he likes is gym. He does not truant because his father has told you that 'he'll beat the crap out of him if he misses school.'

NO NAME GIVEN

Students ask to talk to you confidentially. They tell you that at least one student is having things taken (food and money) by older students. The victim has been threatened and is too frightened to tell. The students indicate that this has happened to some of them but they are alright at the moment. They refuse to say who the culprits are. The victim, who they name, will not admit anything is happening. They give lots of details about the incidents and the threats, but clam up completely when you ask for the name/s of the bully/ies. So you have what, when, where and maybe why, but not who. You think you know who is responsible.

GILL

Gill is new to the school. She has quickly become the leader of a small group of girls. At first several children complained, but now no one says anything. You notice that the children are deferential to Gill and her group. This groups also seems to be 'in charge' of part of the playground. All the other children keep away from an area which they all used to use. This morning a mother telephones to say that her child is very unhappy about coming to school but the child refuses to say why. The mother is distressed and asks to see you as soon as possible. You suspect that this day 'ain't going to be much fun'. Inspectors are due, you are three teachers short, and there is a staff meeting at 3.30pm.

I WAS THE SCHOOL BULLY

I don't really know how to explain things. I never even realised that I had been a bully at school until I was at least 22. One day one of the managers at work told me that his daughter had been at the same school as me. She used to dread meeting me at school and she said that I was well known as the school bully. I'd never really admitted to myself that what I did was bullying. I was horrified.

I had a rotten childhood – my mother was like a witch and I hated her. My parents were always fighting, and my mother picked on me all the time. She used to lie and hit me. It was hell.

I think the bullying started when somebody upset me in the Infants and some of the boys showed me how to make a fist and 'sort her out'. I suppose I just carried on from there. I never used a gang for support and I always picked on girls myself. I'd lie in wait for them on the way home. I used to cat call and fight them – not just pulling hair and scratching but real fighting. I even knocked a girl out once. I was never beaten. Perhaps I would have stopped if somebody had been able to beat me.

I always had an excuse for why I bullied. Things like, 'they were snobs' or 'they'd hurt me' but I know they were pathetic excuses. The lads used to egg me on as well but even when we moved to another area, I still carried on. The bullying went on until I left school.

I never had a feeling of power. I seemed to get satisfaction from knowing that I'd hurt and beaten others but it wasn't power. At heart, I was scared. I thought nobody liked me. I thought I was ugly. I had a big nose and the boys all used to tease me. I felt very insecure.

CHANGING THE BULLY'S BEHAVIOUR: *Exercise 2*

Object: To identify ways you can to help bullies to change their behaviour

Time: 30 minutes

This Exercise focuses on some of the reasons individual bullies might give to explain their actions. It also tries to identify possible ways of helping the bully to change his/her bullying behaviour.

Ask participants to get into pairs. One person to be the bully, the other the teacher. The bully has to think of all the reasons why he/she bullies and the teacher has to think of as many ways as possible of helping the bully change behaviour. Divide a flip chart into two sections, and head them "Why I Bully" and "How to help". Ask pairs to feed back their ideas and write each one in the appropriate column.

The finished chart might look something like the example given on the next page.

When using this Exercise with children and young people, it is useful to sit with them and help them along, if you have the time. Quite often it becomes an opportunity for the bully to discuss his/her problems and to seek help with solutions.

2

Why I Bully	How to Help
* Boredom	* more play equipment in playground/more responsibility or work in the classroom
* Revenge	* examine circumstances/find alternative ways for bully to express feelings
* Envy of victim (clever, sporty)	* praise bully for their own achievements/give bully some extra responsibility to make them feel valued
* Easy target (small, wore glasses)	* roleplay with bully as victim
* Gain status – to establish their position as leader of the group	* peer pressure: bullying, violence and aggression do not grant status but rather diminish it
* Retaliation	* why didn't the bully tell about the first incident? Bullying not an appropriate response in context of whole-school policy
* Anger (bullying a safety valve)	* find out why the bully gets angry and see if anything can be done to prevent anger (for example, bully might be frustrated and angry at not being able to do maths or reading as well as the other children – perhaps extra tuition could help)
* Gain (money, toys, food)	* why does the bully need extra money etc? Does bully get enough money, food from home? Theft not appropriate solution. Roleplays with bully as victim
* It's fun	* sanctions as set out in whole school policy

KIDSCAPE: How to stop bullying

This Exercise indicates some simple ways in which staff can try to influence and change the behaviour of a child who is bullying. Staff can also learn to recognise incidents or circumstances which are likely to trigger bullying behaviour in a particular child (ie. obvious boredom) and can take immediate precautions by diverting the child's attention towards something less explosive!

2

ASSERTIVENESS TRAINING: *Notes and Exercises*

Object: To encourage children and young people to learn assertive, positive
           ways of coping with bullying

Time: 10 to 15 minutes per exercise

The following Exercises are designed to introduce children and young
people, especially those who have been bullied, to new ways of
behaving which will give them strategies for coping with bullying and
with other difficult situations.

They also teach children to think differently about themselves by giving
themselves praise and encouragement. We are grateful to Enid
MacNeill, educational psychologist, who has suggested many of the
following ideas:

BASIC CONCEPTS

1. Assertiveness theory is based on the premise that every individual
   possesses certain basic human rights:

   The right to be treated with respect
   The right to make mistakes and be responsible for them
   The right to refuse requests without having to feel guilty or selfish
   The right to ask for what you want (realising that the other person
       has the right to say no)
   The right to be listened to and to be taken seriously
   The right to say "I don't understand"
   The right to ask for information

These are three possible response styles: passive
                                             aggressive
                                             assertive

Passive people behave as if other people's rights matter more than
theirs.
Aggressive people behave as if their rights matter more than those of
others.
Assertive people respect themselves and others equally.

2. The thoughts we have about ourselves can help or hinder the way
in which we respond to others.
Often we put ourselves down: "No one will like me", "I am hopeless at
this", etc.
We can change this and say helpful things to ourselves instead:
"I have the right to ask for what I want", "I did OK. It wasn't perfect but
it was OK".

TEACHING ASSERTIVENESS SKILLS

Chronic victims and timid or shy children may have poor social skills and might not know how to ask for what they want. Aggressive or boisterous children may just take what they want, or might ask roughly or aggressively.

It is therefore a good idea to do some assertiveness training exercises with the whole class as part of the school campaign to raise awareness of bullying. Assertiveness training teaches all children acceptable ways of behaving. You are most likely wondering where you will get the time to do this, but perhaps you can enlist the help of a volunteer or parent to help the children or young people during break time or after school, if necessary.

EXERCISE 1 – MAKING A REQUEST

First of all, explain that there are three basic rules when making a request:

1. **Be clear about what you want**
2. **Make your request short** (for example, "That is my pencil. I would like it back please".)
3. **Plan and practise** (even if you just go over the request in your own mind)

You have to decide what you are going to say and then stick to it. ("That is my pencil. I want it back".) Don't allow yourself to be side-tracked away from the main issue: it is your pencil and you want it back.

Ask the students to work in pairs. Depending upon their ages and abilities, you may wish to give them a list of requests to practise or have them make up their own. Ask each of the pairs to take turns making a simple, assertive request. Go around the room and comment positively on eye contact, body posture etc.

Possible requests:

I want to turn off the television
I don't want to walk home that way – let's go a different way
I'm not going into that shop
Those shoes do not fit, please bring me a different size
That dog frightens me – I don't want to go near it
I will not give you my homework to copy
I would like you to move please
I am listening to that music – please don't change it
That is my book – please give it to me
Please return my jacket now
I don't want to lend you my watch

EXERCISE 2 – RESPONDING TO BULLYING APPROACHES

When a bully makes a demand, it is sometimes difficult to know what to say. It is a good idea to practise some responses. Ask the children to divide into pairs, one member to play the bully and the other the victim (switching roles frequently). Encourage them to come up with creative responses, but not inflammatory ones:

'Got any sweets on you?'
> 'Yes, but they're horrible. Anyway, I licked them.'
> 'Sorry, they're all gone.'

'Lend us your homework.'
> 'OK, but the teacher has already seen it – I talked to him this morning.'
> 'No, I've not finished it myself.'

'Lend us dinner money.'
> 'Go ahead and have it all, but I'll have to explain to the teacher why I'm so hungry.'
> 'No, borrow it from the teacher, why don't you?'

'We'll be waiting for you after school (at the toilets etc.).'
> 'Fine, should we arrange it with the teacher/Head?'
> 'I would have liked to have been there, but I've got a more important appointment.'

'You've got my book in your bag – I need to look inside it.'
> 'Let's get someone to help then – how about the teacher?'
> 'Your book is not in my bag. Should we go to the Head and sort it out?'

This Exercise will help students to think of what to say, but more importantly, it will help them to stop thinking like a victim even if they never use the little sayings they create.

EXERCISE 3 – THE RIGHT TO SAY NO

If someone is asking you for something which you don't want to agree to, you have the right to say no. It is not selfish to say no and there are occasions when saying no is right for you.

Again, decide what you are going to say and stick to it. Be kind but firm. "I am sorry that you don't have a pencil but I don't want to lend my pencil".

Don't get side-tracked into apologising for your decision or justifying it. Don't make excuses. Keep your body assertive, don't smile and keep good eye-contact. (Sometimes shy children are bad at making eye contact – get them to practise with their families).

If you are not sure what to say, listen to your body and feelings. What do you really want to do? What do you really want to say? You could say something like "I'm not sure. I need more time/more information to decide".

You can offer an alternative: "No, I don't want to play football. Let's go for a walk instead."

Ask the children or young people to work in pairs – different pairs to the previous Exercise, if possible. Either give them a list of possible Saying No statements or have them make up their own:

SAYING NO

No, I don't want to leave right now. But you can go – I'll catch up later.
No, you cannot borrow my gym clothes – sorry.
No, I don't like that.
No, there is no way I can do that.
No, leave me alone, please. I don't want to do that now.
No, it is my book and I need it. Maybe I can help you find one.
No, it just isn't possible for me to go with you. I have too much work to do.
No, you cannot have my chocolate – anyway I've licked it.
No, I cannot loan you any money. I've only got enough for the bus and if I don't come home on it my mother will ring the Head.

EXERCISE 4 – SHOUTING NO

KIDSCAPE teaches children and young people to shout NO as loudly as they can if they are in trouble or danger. The shout should come from the stomach and sound like a fog horn. Practise with the students (and with the staff).

To see if you have taught the students automatically to shout NO very loudly if they are in trouble or are trying to scare someone off, try surprising them while doing one of the other assertiveness training exercises:

Suddenly say 'At the count of three I want you to shout No – One, two, three NOOOOOO!' Good way to wake up a class (and your neighbours – better let them know if this is going to happen).

Exercise 5 – Broken Record Exercise

In this Exercise, children practise saying the same thing over and over again like a broken record. This is a technique which can be used if someone is trying to get round you, or if you are not being listened to, or for saying no.

Ask the children to divide into pairs – make sure bully/ies and victim/s are not together. Ask one child to be A and the other to be B. The children sit down facing their partners.

A has a new bicycle. B wants to borrow it. A doesn't want anyone to play with the new bike. B keeps trying to get the bike from A. Give the children a minute in which B keeps asking for the bike, and A keeps saying No.

At the end of a minute, ask if any of the Bs got the bike? What reasons were given for wanting to borrow the bike? Was it hard for the As to keep saying No?

Repeat the Exercise but this time have A try to borrow B's new football or computer game.

EXERCISE 6 – FOGGING

If we respond to insults with more insults, it builds up. We do not need to do this – we can 'fog'. Fogging swallows up insults like a great fog-bank swallows sights and sounds.

When other people make hurtful remarks, we don't have to argue or become upset; we can turn ourselves into fog and swallow up what they say. If it's true, we respond "that's right". If it's not true, we respond "You could be right" or "It's possible". Don't take the insult personally and keep the answers short and bland.

This may seem very strange at first, but fogging offers an alternative to distress or violence.

This exercise can be done either working in pairs or in a circle. If you work in a circle, you can control the exercise by letting the children or young people send insults to you while you fog them. Make sure that the groundrules are clear and that the exercise doesn't turn into a contest about who can come up with the most horrible insult.

If working in pairs, suggest that each pair has something specific to insult, such as a non-personal item like a pencil or a book:

That is a dumb book
That is such an ugly pencil
That book is written by an idiot
That pencil is an insult to the human race

EXERCISE 7 – RELAXATION

Tense and unhappy children can find it very hard to relax and it is a good idea to teach them the following simple exercise.

Ask the child to lie on the floor. Ask the child to tense every muscle until they feel really rigid. Then ask the child slowly to relax their muscles, starting with their toes and gradually working up to their head. At the end they should be floppy like a rag doll.
(This exercise is great for staff, but can lead to refusal to return to work!)

Ask them to repeat the exercise three times.

EXERCISE 8 – WAYS OF LEARNING TO BE ASSERTIVE

Help children learn to be assertive by giving them the chance to practise the new skills in a safe and supportive atmosphere.

Ask them "what if" questions (What would you do if a bully came up to you in the playground and started calling you names? What would you do if a bully cornered you in the lavatories and asked for your money? See SECTION 3 WHAT IF? QUESTIONS for a list of questions you can use with children). You can help them work out the best course of action and they can practise different responses.

Talk about situations the child finds difficult. Teach them that they cannot change what has happened in the past but they can learn from it. Discuss particular incidents with the child. Could they have behaved differently? Said or done something else? Would it have made the situation better or worse?

Discuss what they could do if the same thing happened again. Discuss different strategies and ways of coping which are possible for the child and practice them in roleplays.

See the What if? questions listed in this guide or have the children make up their own.

EXERCISE 9 – POSTURE

Chronic victims often have poor posture and tend to creep about. They need to learn how to stand up straight, how to walk confidently, how to make and keep eye-contact. Get them to practise in front of a mirror.

They need to learn how other people behave. Get the child to pretend to be a detective. They should watch other people, look at eye-contact, look at the way people stand, the way they walk, listen to their tone of voice, listen to what they say. Ask them to decide what is passive, what is aggressive and what is assertive behaviour. They could write a report on someone they have been studying (warn them not to stare bug-eyed at some unsuspecting acquaintance!).

2

KIDSCAPE: How to stop bullying

CHANGING THE WAY YOU COMMUNICATE: *Notes and Exercise*

Bullies and victims get set in their patterns of communication. One way to help them to change is to give them specific suggestions which they can practise.

For example, Lisa has been a victim of bullying for several months. She has taken the bullying to heart and now sees herself as a victim. When she talks to people, she hangs her head and is quite hesitant. She starts her sentences in an apologetic way: 'I'm sorry, but do you think you could.......?'

Gill, on the other hand, has got away with bullying other children for years. When she wants something, she begins with 'You, come here' or 'I want you to.....'

Both of these girls need to learn more positive and effective ways of communicating so that they can begin to change their behaviour.

There are several steps to learning to communicate more effectively:

● Getting the attention of the other person or persons in a good way
 – not by interrupting or by being nasty or by apologising for living

● Looking at the person you are talking to

● Ensuring that you are talking with the appropriate level of sound –
 not too loud and demanding or too soft and self-effacing

● Being efficient with your words – don't use twenty words
 when ten will do

● Making your request clearly

EXERCISE: EFFECTIVE COMMUNICATION

Object: Learning to speak to people effectively

Time: 20 minutes

Needed: Two people or one person with a mirror

Think of a simple request you would like to make, such as 'Could you please help me with my maths?', or 'Would you like to come over to my house after school?' or 'Stop that – I don't like it.'

1) Face the other person (or the mirror)

2) Think of a pleasant thought and relax your face – you don't have to smile, but it helps if you can

3) Make sure you have eye contact, but don't 'stare him/her down' – this is not a power contest. Your look should be friendly, unless you are trying to convey displeasure

4) State your question or request in a firm, friendly voice – don't shout or whisper

5) Don't beg, plead or demand – say clearly what you mean:

> 'Would you please help me with my maths? I don't understand this problem.'

> 'I would like you to come over on Saturday, if you can. Perhaps we could go to the cinema?'

> 'That ball is meant to be shared by all of us. Let's start the game again.'

> 'I said no and I mean no.'

> 'Go away and leave me alone.'

> 'I'd love to. It sounds like fun.'

6) End the conversation when you are ready:

'Got to get to class. See you.'

'Thanks a lot. Talk to you later.'

'You've been a big help. Thanks. 'Bye.'

'There's no point in talking further. Good bye.'

'We'll just have to agree to disagree.'

'I look forward to seeing you Saturday, ten o'clock.'

DEALING WITH ANGER: *Notes and Four Exercises*

Bullies and victims may be full of anger. Often bullies turn their anger outward and attack someone, even though the victim chosen was not the original cause of their anger. Victims turn their anger towards themselves or perhaps towards a family member, even though they are angry with the bully. Both bullies and victims may need help to manage their anger in a more constructive way.

EXERCISE:

2

Object: To help bullies and victims think about constructive ways to deal with anger

Time: 20 minutes

Materials: Paper and pens

Ask the participants to break into small groups. Ask the groups to brainstorm and come up with a list of reasons which answer the following questions. (Also listed are suggestions that KIDSCAPE groups have put together in case you need some 'trigger' statements – which you may or may not agree with.)

● Why do people get angry?

Because they don't get what they want
Because they are frustrated
Because they cannot do their school work
Because they are hurt and afraid to show it
Because they feel hard done by
Because they feel frightened or inadequate
Because they are being abused and can't tell
Because they are used to getting their own way

● When is anger OK?

If something is unfair
If someone is being harmed
If dictators are killing people
If someone is being bullied
If someone is being called racist names
If people have been abused

● When is anger not OK?

> If it is used to hurt someone
> If it is used unfairly
> If it is used to gain power over someone
> If it makes you sick
> If it is turned against yourself

● How can anger be expressed?

> * State the reasons for your anger calmly and be specific: 'I'm angry because you didn't meet me at the cinema like you promised'.

> * State what you would like to happen to remedy the situation: 'You owe me an apology' or 'I expect you to replace the toy you broke'.

> * Listen to what the other person says without interrupting.

> * Stick to the current problem – don't bring up all the sins of the past, such as 'You're always doing that'.

> * Try not to use blame – better to say 'It makes me angry when you take my video game without asking', not 'You're a terrible person for taking my game and I hate you'.

FOLLOW-UP EXERCISE 1

Divide the group into pairs. Ask each pair to think of a time in their lives when they were really angry about something, but the situation was not handled as they would have wished. It might have been a time when a brother or sister got 'away with murder' or a time they were blamed for something they didn't do or a time when they felt they were not treated fairly at home or at school.

Working in pairs, give each person three minutes to tell their story. The listener must not interrupt, but should listen intently and show interest. At the end of three minutes, the other person tells his/her story, with the listener not interrupting.

KIDSCAPE: How to stop bullying

After each person has told their story, they can then ask each other any questions about what happened.

Then the pairs could discuss the following:

● What other feelings did they feel besides anger?

● What was the most upsetting thing about the situation?

● What solutions might work for each situation? For example, would humour help? Would it help to sit down with the person who caused the anger and talk it through? Would it help to meet with a third party and negotiate? Would it help just to let go of the anger and to stop focusing on it?

2 FOLLOW-UP EXERCISE 2

Ask the students to compile a list of the ways they think people express anger indirectly, such as:

Using drugs or alcohol
Overeating
Starving themselves (Anorexia)
Deliberately failing
Getting sick
Becoming depressed
Self mutilating

Ask the students:

Who is hurt when anger comes out indirectly?
How they would counsel someone who was exhibiting signs of indirect anger?
To write or dramatise a story about someone who is angry and doesn't show it directly – the story or drama should include a better way to deal with it.

FOLLOW-UP EXERCISE 3

Ask the students to make up an 'I feel angry' Questionnaire that can be filled in. For example:

I feel angry when ....

....

I wish I could say to someone I feel angry with ....

....

There are times when I feel like ....

....

Anger is good when ....

....

Anger is bad when ....

....

I wish that .... would not be angry with me

If I tell someone I am angry, they will ....

....

The way I express my anger is ....

....

When I get angry I ....

....

I think the most positive way to deal with being angry is

....

KIDSCAPE: How to stop bullying

Ask the students to complete the Questionnaire. Depending upon the group, you may then wish to:

- Allow them to keep their answers and ask them to write a paragraph on 'Dealing with Anger'

- Lead a group discussion on the points in the questionnaire (don't let it focus on individuals)

- Meet individually with students to discuss their answers and to make suggestions

- Ask them to discuss their answers in pairs or in small groups

2

MY SPACE: *Exercise*

Object: To help students recognise that people have a right to their own personal space and that 'invading' someone's space can be threatening

Time: 20 minutes

Needed: Even number of students

Divide the students into two groups. Ask the two groups to face one another across the room. Try to have as much space as possible between the groups, but ensure that they can see one another. Have each group member mutually identify a person opposite as 'their person'. Give each group a number or letter or name, such as:

Groups A & B
Groups 1 & 2
Groups Blue and Red

Decide which group you will ask to move forward (we'll say A) and which group will stand still as the other group approaches them (we'll say B). Group B should be told that they should put their hand out when they feel 'their' person in the advancing Group A has come too close to them. Each person in Group A must stop when their opposite number in Group B holds out his/her hand.

Begin:

When you give the signal, Group A (or 1 or Red) moves slowly across the room – each member of group A targeting their opposite number in group B. Gradually members of Group A will stop as their opposite numbers put out their hands.

When all Group A members have been stopped:

See how the distances vary. It is interesting that some people can tolerate quite 'close encounters,' while others don't want anyone within a mile.

Discuss how people feel when someone 'invades their space':

Is some bullying caused because the bully lashes out if someone comes too close?

Are victims sometimes over-sensitive about people coming into their space and do they over-react?

How can we be sensitive to each other to ensure that no one feels threatened by 'space invasion'?

2

KIDSCAPE: How to stop bullying

ABOUT YOURSELF QUESTIONNAIRE: *Exercise*

Object: To help children and young people who have been bullied or who have bullied others to start to think about their positive attributes and to help them to develop a better self-image

Time: 20 minutes

Materials: Copies of Questionnaire

This Questionnaire can be adapted for students, depending upon their age and ability. It is a good tool for the adults working with victims and/or students who have bullied because it may give information which can be used to build a child's self-confidence and esteem. If a child doesn't think there is anything about him/her that people like, it would be a step forward if you could find even one positive thing to say the next time they fill in the Questionnaire or, if they have no goals, help them to think of one – like finding one thing about themselves to like.

It is also useful to give the Questionnaire after working with a child or young person with the other Exercises in this section to see if their self image has changed and, hopefully, improved. The Questionnaire can be used at intervals of 3 to 6 months to note changes.

Suggested Questionnaire:

Name .... Date ....

What are your favourite television programmes? ....

....

What are your favourite sports, music, hobbies, activities? ....

....

Name 5 good things about yourself ....

....

List 5 words that best describe you ....

....

List 5 words that describe your family ....

....

What do you like to do most? ....

What do you like to do least? ....

Who is your best friend? ....

What is it about friends that you most value? ....

....

What is it that makes people like you? ....

....

List 5 things you would like to do by the time you are 21 ....

....

....

List 5 things you would like to do by the time you are 40 ....

....

....

What do you like/dislike about school? ....

....

How would you change school if you had a magic wand? ....

....

How would you change yourself if you had a magic wand? ....

....

ICE-BREAKER – GETTING TO KNOW PEOPLE: *Exercise*

2

Object: To help groups of children or young people who are working on the problem of bullying to start to develop a trusting environment and the confidence to talk to each other

Time: 15 minutes

It is difficult for students to feel comfortable in a new group, especially if that group will be dealing with the problem of bullying.

Divide the group into pairs. Ask each person to tell their partner as much as possible about themselves. Give each person about 5 minutes. You may use ideas from the 'About Yourself' Questionnaire (see previous Exercise) to give them a trigger, if they cannot think of how to begin. After each person has talked, ask the students to come back together in the larger group.

Ask each student to introduce their partner by giving the partner's name and the two things that impressed them the most about their partner.

Discuss with the group how it felt to talk to one person and how it felt to talk in front of a larger group.

Ensure that the students realise that what is said in the pairs or in the group is confidential and not to be discussed outside.

Alternately, if you have a small group, you can ask the students to go around and introduce themselves by saying three or four good things about themselves.

ALL ABOUT ME: Exercise

Object: To help students learn about each other and/or to help an adult working with the group to understand them better

Time: 15 minutes

Materials: List of Questions below or questions of your own

The students can work in pairs, in small groups or individually (to help you gather information to help each student). Give the students the following List of Questions or make up your own questions. In pairs or small groups, have them each answer a question in turn and then go on to the next question. Individually, you can give each person the questions and ask them to write the answers or go over the questions with the students and discuss the answers with them.

List of Questions:

1. What have you done that makes you most proud/happy?

2. What was/is your nickname? Do you like it? Is there a nickname you'd like to be called?

3. Do you like your name? Would you change it? To what?

4. What is the best thing that has ever happened to you?

5. What is the weirdest thing that has ever happened to you?

6. What is the silliest thing that you ever did?

7. What is the funniest thing that ever happened to you?

8. What is the saddest thing that ever happened to you?

9. What person do you most admire? Why?

10. What qualities do you look for in a friend?

11. What is your best quality?

12. What is your worst quality?

13. What is the most important thing in your life?

14. Who is the most important person in your life?

15. What one thing would you change about yourself?

16. What one thing would you change about your family?

17. What one thing would you change about this class/school?

18. What do you hate doing most in the whole world?

19. What do you like doing most in the whole world?

20. If you could be anyone in the whole world, who would you be and why?

2

HAPPY THOUGHTS: *Exercise*

Object: To help the students relax and think of being successful which might help to raise their self-image

Time: 5 to 10 minutes

Ask the students to relax and close their eyes. If you are working with a small group (and the floor is clean!), ask the students to lie on the floor. Otherwise have them sit as comfortably as possible, either in chairs or on cushions.

Tell them to think of watching a film and to imagine that the film is about them. Ask them to remember a happy time in their lives and to 'see' that time on the film. Where did they live, what did they eat, who did they play with or go out with, what did it 'feel' like to be happy then?

Ask them to think of something good that they did during that happy time – some success they had. It might have been with friends, with school work, with music or sports, with family, with a pet – anything. Did they tell anyone about the success? Were they praised for it? How did it feel to do something successfully?

Ask the students to try to think about themselves as successful and positive. Explain that often, because people only think negative things about themselves, they tear themselves to pieces. It may be harder to think about being positive and being successful, but this is exactly the frame of mind that helps people to start changing how they look at themselves.

Ask the students to open their eyes gradually and to talk about how it feels to be successful. Ask them to think of one way they might try to succeed in the next week – perhaps by avoiding bullying someone, or by being more humorous, or by making a light-hearted comment instead of taking something too seriously, or by walking away instead of fighting.

Ask the students to report back in one week and share their success with the group.

2

KIDSCAPE: How to stop bullying

I AM PROUD THAT ...... : *Exercise*

Object: To help students express pride about something they have done in order to increase their self-confidence

Time: 15 minutes

Materials: List of Suggestions below or your own suggestions, magazines, paper, glue for follow-up exercises

Ask the students to complete the following statements with something they are proud of doing. They can do the Exercise either in a group or individually.

I am proud that:

* For a friend I have ....

....

* For my sister/brother I have ....

....

* For my parents I have ....

....

* I tried very hard to ....

....

* I did well in ....

....

* I did not ....

....

* I am good at ....

....

* For myself I ....

....

* I helped ....

....

* I always ....

....

* I have improved at ....

....

* I will become ....

....

* My greatest achievement is ....

....

* My most exciting ambition is to ....

....

FOLLOW-UP EXERCISE:

Design a flag or coat of arms using some of your 'proud' statements

Design a Proud Motto about yourself

Make an 'I am Proud' collage using magazine pictures or your own drawings

COLLAGE MAKING: *Exercise*

Object: To help students think about bullying

Time: 30 minutes

Materials: A variety of magazines (lots) with pictures to cut out, paper to paste pictures on, glue, scissors

Collages are a non-threatening way for students to express their feelings about bullying.

Ask the students to work on a 'bullying' theme to make collages. They go through the magazines and cut or tear out pictures which reflect the theme. Some suggestion for themes are:

* When I am bullied I feel............

* When I see someone being bullied......

* People who bully are.......................

* Victims are....................

* What I would like to do to people who bully....

* How people who bully feel..............

* How victims feel..............

* What adults do about bullying......................

* Bullying is.........................

* Ways to stop bullying.....................................

* The way I see myself......................................

* The way others see me....................................

* The way I wish I was..

* The way parents/teachers/students see me........

PUT DOWNS: *Exercise*

Object: Looking at 'put downs' and thinking about positive ways to interact with others. This Exercise is particularly useful for children and young people who bully others using hurtful words and gestures

Time: 60 minutes

Ask the students to think of all the 'put down' comments people make. Write some of them on the board:

You're stupid
Why did you do it *that* way?
Too bad about the face
Go back where you came from
Get that shirt from Oxfam?
Like your hair – NOT
That's gay
Look who's escaped from the zoo
That was a dumb idea
You couldn't even do *that* right

Also ask them to think of gestures or facial expressions that are 'put downs' such as:

Holding your nose
Making monkey-like gestures and noises
Rolling your eyes
Letting your mouth hang open in a 'you're dumb' expression
Making 'you're crazy' circles next to your ear

As a project, ask the students to spend some time observing others on the playground or in the dining room and noting comments, gestures and facial expressions which could be considered 'put downs'. Ask them to make a list – be sure that they know they can include members of staff in their observations (some of the most sarcastic comments have been known to come from staff! See SECTION 1). However, this Exercise is about collecting information, and is not about naming culprits.

You can also ask the students to gather information from home and other places outside school.

When the students have completed their assignment, ask them to get into small groups and compile lists in the following three categories:

* Comments
* Gestures
* Expressions

Then discuss with the students why people hide behind hurtful, sarcastic 'put downs'. Ask them how they think people feel when they are put down. See if any of the students will themselves own up to having used 'put downs'. Discuss other, more positive ways of relating to other people.

Try to compile a 'Build Up' list, such as:

That was a good try
Nevermind, you'll get it eventually
I guess that idea didn't work
It doesn't matter
I like your trainers

Ask the students to note every time they stop themselves putting someone down and whenever they find a nicer way of relating to other people. This can be for a day, a week or for a short time in the case of students who seem to put others down all the time. For these students, it might be more realistic to ask them to be 'nice' for 10 minutes!

Discuss with students how they have succeeded or, if they haven't, perhaps other students could help them by acting as monitors and giving suggestions. It isn't easy to change, but it can help the child or young person who is bullying to learn how to interact more positively, including learning to smile or at least not to glower. Give lots of reinforcement when students succeed in finding new ways of acting.

170

NO MATTER WHAT: Exercise

Object: To help victims of bullying think positively about themselves and/or have something to say in their heads to counter negative comments from others

Time: 10 minutes

This is a counselling Exercise and should only be used when students know the other group members well and when they trust each other.

Ask the students to repeat silently to themselves while you say aloud ten times: 'No matter what you say, I'm a good person'. Then ask them to say it aloud with you several times – loudly and with feeling:

'NO MATTER WHAT YOU SAY, I'M A GOOD PERSON'.

Vary this with 'I don't deserve this' and 'I deserve to be treated better than this' and other statements relevant to the group you are working with.

Ask the students to close their eyes and to imagine a time when someone said something to them that was unfair, that they didn't deserve. Give them a minute to call up the face of the person, then say together loudly: 'NO MATTER WHAT YOU SAY, I'M A GOOD PERSON.' Have the students say it three times, each time more loudly than the last (warn your neighbours!)

Repeat the Exercise using different images and responses. Ask the students to use strong body language such as standing up, throwing out their chests, shoulders back, putting their hands on their hips, etc. (you can ask them to stand like a hero or heroine). For students with special needs, use as many gestures or stances as possible – if the students sign, help them to sign 'with attitude'; if they are in a wheelchair and can control their upper bodies, ask them to thrust their chins out and look determined.

2

The object is to build confidence and to develop a protective mind set so that if people say hurtful things they bounce off. As the students gain confidence, you could have them respond to your comments such as:

* You're stupid
* You look funny in those glasses
* Guess you forgot to put on your face today
* Nice dress – too bad about the body
* Pimple-face
* Ugly
* Think you're smart?

– with a loud: 'NO MATTER WHAT YOU SAY, I'M A GOOD PERSON'.

Make sure the students you are working with understand that you are insulting them as part of the Exercise. Some of them may find that their defensive mind sets are not as strong as they thought once they start to hear derogatory comments actually being addressed to them. Tread cautiously!

You may wish to do this Exercise with individual students.

Help the students to develop protective statements they can say to themselves if faced with hostility.

PAT ON THE BACK: *Exercise*

Object: To build up feelings of self-worth

Time: 15 minutes

Materials: None for Main Exercise, but you will need photographs of students for Follow-up Exercise and/or paper, scissors, paste and an overhead projector or other strong light source for the other Follow-up Exercise

This Exercise can only work in a group where the members feel quite comfortable about sharing feelings and where they know each other quite well. If you are working with a group of children or young people who are still unsure of each other, put this Exercise on the back burner until they are ready.

Ask the students to focus on one person at a time. One other student or the adult acts as recorder and takes down everything that is said. The remaining students say positive and only positive statements about the student who is in focus, such as:

Kind to others
Fun
Smiles alot
Good at maths
Understanding
Loves pets
Never hits anyone

The recorder writes it down and gives it to the person to keep. The another student records and someone else is in focus. This can act as a salve for emotionally wounded students who feel they are no good – to hear others saying nice things is quite wonderful even if you don't really believe everything that is being said... yet!

FOLLOW-UP EXERCISES:

* Put up a picture of each student and ask everyone to write something good about each person (best done under supervision if you've got students who are intent on being nasty – or in small groups with students who completely trust each other)

*   Cut out silhouettes of each student (easily done if you are talented in art – if, like me you aren't, then cheat by standing the student between an overhead projector and a piece of paper, trace an outline of the student's shadow (face), cut it out and mount it on another piece of paper (coloured if you have it).

Then write one good thing about that student on the silhouette, post it in the room and ask other students to add their good comments. You can do this using one silhouette a day or using them all for one lesson. The advantage of putting up one a day is that that student becomes the focus of lots of positive feelings and doesn't have to share the limelight.

Allow the students to keep their photo-compliments and silhouettes after they have been displayed and taken down.

2

KIDSCAPE: How to stop bullying

PLAN OF ACTION: *Exercise*

Object: To set realistic goals and to change behaviour

Time: 30 minutes

Children and young people caught up in bullying may benefit from working out how to take control of themselves and to think about where they are going.

Help the students to think of ways to make a plan. It might be done in steps, such as:

1. Learn about yourself – am I happy with the way things are going? If not, what can I do to change things?

2. I'm responsible – if I am doing something to make myself or others unhappy, then it is my responsibility to change.

3. What can I do? – what will happen if I continue on this path? What choices do I have? – make a list. What one thing can I work on today, this week, this year?

4. Plan it out – what will I do/say when I see the person I am bullying or what will I do/say if I see the person who is bullying me? How will I change this relationship? Write it down, step by step. Some students have written things like:

   ★ I will not go to where I know s/he is
   ★ If we come face to face I will not say anything and will just walk away
   ★ I will not hit/kick during break-time
   ★ I will wait to go home until after the person I have bullied has had lots of time to get home
   ★ I will smile when I see ....
   ★ I won't allow .... to wind me up
   ★ If she says that again, I will say to myself: 'No matter what you say, I know I'm a good person'

5. Evaluate how the plan worked – how did you feel? What else could you have done? Did what you do help the situation or make it worse? What will you try next? Use the following Exercise, A Good Week, to help you to evaluate your progress, as well.

A GOOD WEEK: *Exercise*

Object: For students who are trying to overcome having a victim mentality or bullying others (or a combination of both) this is a way to self-evaluate progress

Time: 10 minutes

Materials: Copy of 'Weekly Progress' sheet below

Each student has his/her own sheet, which can be adapted for their particular situation. *If a student is fragile, this Exercise may not be appropriate because the student may feel s/he has not made not progress and it could be depressing, so use with care.*

Each week give each student a blank copy of the Weekly Progress sheet and ask them to fill it out privately. Alternately, you can use this as an opportunity to work with the student and fill it out together. By looking at the sheets over a month, the students can see where they've progressed and what they might want to work on.

Name .... Date ....

1. What is the nicest thing that happened to you this week?

....

....

2. What was the worst thing that happened? ....

....

3. What was the best thing you did (or said to) for someone?

....

4. What was the best thing you did for yourself? ....

....

5. Name one thing you changed ....

....

6. What did you learn about yourself? ....

....

7. How could this week have been improved? ....

....

8. My goal for next week is ....

....

2

LABELS: *Exercise*

Object: To help students think about how damaging it is to label themselves

Time: 20 minutes

When children and young people are labelled as bad or stupid or a bully, these often become self-fulfilling prophecies. The student thinks s/he is a bully or dumb and acts accordingly. If we can help students to see that their *behaviour* might be bad, but that *they are not bad*, it may help them to assess what they are doing and then try and change.

Ask the students to write down one or two negative things people call each other (or, with a group that is secure about working with each other, ask them to write down something about themselves). Take things like bad, bully, stupid, ugly, etc. and write the words in a column on the board without identifying the source (don't use general descriptions like 'red hair' or 'wears glasses' as these are not negative comments):

Bad

Bully

Stupid

Then help the students to think aloud of less damaging ways to describe the behaviour without labelling the person:

Label	Alternative
Bad	'I sometimes fight with other kids – that's bad, but I can change that behaviour.'
Bully	'I said some really nasty things to someone yesterday – that was bullying. I'm going to stop bullying.'
Stupid	'I'm not very good at fractions, but I do understand how to multiply – I guess I'm not stupid, I just don't understand that bit. I'm better at English than Maths, anyway.'

Students need to understand that they may do bad things, or bully or be slow in something, but that doesn't mean they need to be bad, bullies or stupid all the time.

Ask the students to keep a record of all the times during the day that they or someone else tells them something bad about themselves and then work with them to re-think and re-write those thoughts and words in a less damaging way.

KIDSCAPE: How to stop bullying

BULLYING TEACHES US: *Exercise*

Object: To help students understand what might cause some children to bully

Time: 45 minutes

Materials: Copies of poems in this Exercise

Give the students a copy of the wonderful poem 'Children Learn What They Live' by Dorothy Law Nolte:

Children Learn What They Live

Dorothy Law Nolte

If a child lives with criticism,
    he learns to condemn.
If a child lives with hostility,
    he learns to fight.
If a child lives with fear,
    he learns to be apprehensive.
If a child lives with pity,
    he learns to feel sorry for himself.
If a child lives with ridicule,
    he learns to be shy.
If a child lives with jealousy,
    he learns what envy is.
If a child lives with shame,
    he learns to feel guilty.

If a child lives with encouragement,
    he learns to be confident.
If a child lives with tolerance,
    he learns to be patient.
If a child lives with praise,
    he learns to be appreciative.
If a child lives with acceptance,
    he learns to love.
If a child lives with approval,
    he learns to like himself.
If a child lives with recognition,
    he learns that it is good to have a goal.
If a child lives with sharing,
    he learns about generosity.

If a child lives with honesty and fairness,
    he learns what truth and justice are.
If a child lives with security,
    he learns to have faith in himself and in those about him.
If a child lives with friendliness,
    he learns that the world is a nice place in which to live.
If you live with serenity,
    your child will have peace of mind.

Ask the students to think about the poem and about how it relates to them. Have they learned negative things which they can work on 'unlearning'? What positive things have they learned? How would they bring up their children?

Ask the students to come up with a version of this poem, using bullying as a theme. For example;

Bullying Teaches Us

If a child is bullied at home,
    s/he learns ....
If a child is bullied by other students,
    s/he learns ....
If a child is labelled as a bully,
    s/he learns ....
If a child bullies others,
    s/he learns ....
If a child ask for help and no one does anything,
    s/he learns ....
If a child is told s/he is stupid,
    s/he learns ....
If a child is not stopped from bullying,
    s/he learns ....
If a child tells about bullying and it gets worse,
    s/he learns ....
If a child has a teacher who is a bully,
    s/he learns ....
If a child gets away with bullying for a long time,
    s/he learns ....
If bullying goes on and other children see it,
    they learn ....
If bullying is not stopped,
    we all learn ....

MAKING FRIENDS: *Exercise*

Object: To help students learn ways to make friends

Time: 30 minutes

Although we ask students to become friends, we seldom help them to think of how to go about it. Bullying is sometimes the result of misguided attempts by children or young people trying to become part of a group or trying to approach someone to make friends.

Ask the students to discuss ways to make friends. Have them work in small groups and come up with a list of ten ways to make a friend. Then ask them to report to the larger group and write the suggestions on the board, avoiding duplication.

These suggestions were compiled by a group of 13 year olds:

* Showing an interest in what people do
* Being complimentary without going overboard
* Having a pleasant expression on your face
* Laughing at people's jokes
* Being kind
* Asking to join in
* Offering to help
* Inviting people to do something
* Going to places where other students are
* Being welcoming to new students
* Bringing something interesting to do
* Being willing to share
* Being humorous/telling jokes
* Being fair
* Organising games or activities
* Thinking of new ideas

Using the same method, ask the students to think about ways NOT to make friends. One group thought of the following:

* Being bossy
* Telling others how to play
* Telling others they are doing things wrong
* Talking about yourself all the time
* Being mean
* Talking about other students behind their backs
* Being negative and sarcastic
* Being too intense or serious all the time
* Bragging

*   Moaning all the time
*   Being a bully
*   Claiming credit for something you didn't do
*   Lying or cheating

Ask the students to draw up a Friendship Charter and display it in the school where it can be seen and discussed.

FOLLOW-UP EXERCISES:

Ask the students to roleplay someone trying to make friends the wrong way and then another roleplay showing the right way.

Ask the students to conduct a survey asking students and staff for their ideas on making friends. Chart the results and discuss.

Write a paper about an imaginary new student trying to make friends in your school – what obstacles might s/he encounter? What things would help? Include suggestions which the school might use to change for the better.

CORNUCOPIA OF IDEAS FOR EXERCISES

Object: To give the beleaguered teacher or staff member some quick ideas to use in a pinch or to round off a lesson about bullying.

Dip in and out of this section – most of the ideas have come from participants on KIDSCAPE workshops, who have used them with their own students:

1. **Story/Play** – ask older children to read a story or prepare a short play about bullying for younger children.

2. **Letter** – ask the students to write a letter to a pen pal describing what they like to do, what kind of a person they are, what they hope to do when they leave school. This can either be to a real pen pal or to an imaginary one.

3. **Body Outline** – for younger children, get them to lie down on a large piece of paper (rolls of heavy lining paper from a DIY shop are perfect for this and quite cheap) and trace an outline of their bodies. Ask the children to cut out their outline and colour it in as they wish. Get a pad of Post-it notes and write something good about each child and attach the note to the outline, perhaps on the hand. Change the message as often as possible – the children will be delighted.

4. **Nicknames** – ask the students what nickname they would like to be called if they had a choice. Often hurtful nicknames are given to children and young people and then used to bully them. Help each student find a positive nickname for him/herself. This might be a good opportunity to use words from other languages, such as Solecito (Spanish for little sun), Shaina (Yiddish for beautiful), Leoncito (Spanish for little lion). Ask the students for other suggestions. Come up with a list and let the students decide on their own names, but don't let anyone pick a negative nickname.

5. **Student of the Week** – each week put up the picture of one student. Ask each of the other students to say one good thing about the student and make a list of 5 statements to put under the picture. If you want to speed up the exercise, have a Student of the Day. Try to have all the pictures and comments up on Parents' Evening and ask the parents to add a comment (if all the parents can't come, try to get a good comment either in writing or over the telephone and add it to the child's list).

6. **Poem** – ask the students to write a poem about bullying.

7. **Perfect School** – ask the students to design a perfect school in which everyone is happy and there is no bullying. This can be a drawing, a story or a combination of both.

8. **Positive/Negative** – ask the students to draw a line down the centre of a piece of paper and write Positive at the top on one side and Negative on the other. Ask them to write in three positive things about themselves in the first column and three negative things in the second. The groundrule is that none of the traits can be physical, but should be things that have been developed by the student and therefore could be changed. For example:

Positive	Negatives
Honest	Bad temper
Fast runner	Don't do homework
Like pets	Untidy

Ask the students if they could work on changing one negative trait into a positive one over the next week or month. This Exercise is best done individually and not with other students unless a trusting relationship has been built up; otherwise the 'negatives' could be used to bully.

9. **Class Newsletter** – ask each student to contribute an article, drawing, puzzle, or poem about bullying to a class newsletter. Have the students put the newsletter together and photocopy it for parents, students and staff.

10. **Millionaire** – tell the students that they have each inherited £1,000,000, of which they must use 90% to eradicate bullying. After they have stopped all bullying, they can then use the remaining 10% of the money for personal use and must use that 10% to make their own lives happier. How would they use the money? The students can either work individually and write about what they would do or work in small groups and report back to the class what they would do as a group.

11. **Puppet Play** – using socks decorated by children (buttons for eyes, felt mouths, wool for hair and whiskers) or paper cut-outs of characters, ask the children to make up a puppet play about a child who is being bullied and how sad the child feels. Ask them to think of a positive way to end the play so that the child who is bullying gets help and so does the victim – a happy ending!

12. **Mural** – ask the students to co-operate on drawing and decorating a class mural depicting on one panel a playground where bullying is happening and on another panel a playground where everyone is having a good time and where there is no bullying. Discuss your own playground and think of ways which could make it more like the 'No bullying' panel.

13. **Make Someone Feel Good** – ask the students to agree to each do or say at least one thing a day to make someone else feel good. Have a rule that it has to be a different person each day that they make feel good. You may want to make this a month-long project and ask each student to do or say something to each member of the class or group. Ask each student to keep a journal or record of what they do and discuss it with them.

14. **Wish List** – ask students to write down on one side of paper 5 words which describe them. On the other side of the paper write down 5 words which they wished described them.

   Ask them to take one of the words on their Wish List and describe what it means to be like that. For example, if they said they wished they were 'happy', what does it mean to them to be happy?

   People who seem to be happy:

   Smile
   Have friends
   Do well in school
   Have money
   Come from nice families
   Feel good about themselves

   Then ask the students to look at the list they have just made to see which things it might be possible for them to work on to become happy. It might not be possible to have money (or necessarily even true that you need it to be happy) or to come from a nice family, but it might be possible to work on smiling, having friends, doing well in school and feeling good about themselves.

   Ask the students to make it a goal to work on attaining at least one of the ideals on their Wish List. Help them work out an action plan to achieve their goal: for example, if the goal is to 'be popular', then the student needs to think about how they can make friends and adopt welcoming and friendly behaviour (See MAKING FRIENDS EXERCISE). Their action plan might start something like this:

   ★ Try to smile at people whenever possible
   ★ Be kind to other people and helpful

2

* Invite someone home
* Be ready to listen to others

For 'Doing well in school', the action plan might look like this:

* Choose one subject to work on to start with
* Ask the teacher for extra help
* Set aside more time to work on that subject
* Study with someone who might be able to help you understand it better
* Don't get discouraged if it takes some time to get better in the subject
* Tell yourself that you will improve and believe that you can do it
* Ignore anyone who attempts to discourage you, even a well meaning parent who says, 'I never did very well in that either'
* Reward yourself for getting better

This Exercise helps people to develop self-esteem if they follow through and actually are able to change the goal from a wish to a reality. Although it does take lots of help and encouragement, it is worth it to achieve the goal. The students can do this Exercise with parents and other adults if they are supportive.

15. **Bully Gang** – ask the students to write a story about a child or young person who suddenly finds that they are being pulled into a bully gang and being pressured to start bullying a person they have been friends with in the past. Ask them to write about what the character might be thinking and feeling and how s/he resolves the problem. Use these stories as a springboard to discuss how hard it is to resist peer pressure and how many people who bully others might not really want to but are frightened or led into this type behaviour and how they can get help to stop.

16. **Victim Viewpoint** – after the students have completed the Exercise above, ask them to write the same story from the viewpoint of the victim. S/he will be confused, frightened and worried, especially when one of her/his friends joins in the gang bullying. Again follow this with discussion about how the victims of bullying can feel and how they can get help.

17. **Bulletin Board** – ask students to look for references to bullying, including racist attacks or attacks on gay or lesbian people or incidents of suicide or suicide attempts attributed to bullying in the press over a month and use these stories to create a bulletin board and to discuss the issue of bullying and ideas about stopping it.

KIDSCAPE: How to stop bullying

18. **Mystery Person** – give each student the name of another student and tell them to keep the name of their student a secret. Ask them to telephone each other or talk away from school to their student to find out 'different' facts about them – not just biographical details but names of pets, kinds of food they like, secret ambitions, etc. Have the students write about their Mystery Person without giving their name, then read aloud their writing to see if the class can guess who the person is. Start with general information like:

My Mystery Person loves chocolate ice cream and Chinese Food (not mixed together). My Mystery Person secretly wants to become a famous rock star and dye his/her hair blue.

My Mystery Person likes to go swimming in the holidays. S/he nearly got run over by a car when s/he was 3 years old.

My Mystery Person likes to draw, make plasticine models and take things apart to see how they work.

My Mystery Person is known to smile a lot.

My Mystery Person has 2 brothers, a cat, a dog and a gerbil. S/he likes the pets, but sometimes can't stand the brothers.

My Mystery Person has brown hair and brown eyes and is 5 feet 6 inches tall. Who is s/he?

At various points before the end of the reading, ask the students to raise their hands if they think they know who the Mystery Person is – the comments being read out should all be positive (you may wish to check the stories) and gradually get specific so that the identity of the Mystery Person becomes apparent. This is a good way to focus positively on a student, making them the centre of attention in a nice way and revealing new information about him/her which might be interesting.

19. **Dear Bully Letter** – ask the students to write a letter to an imaginary bully to try to explain why s/he should try to change and give some suggestions on how to change.

20. **Dear Bullied Person Letter** – ask the students to write to an imaginary victim of bullying telling the victim how they will personally help him/her to stop being a victim and giving advice about how the victim might get some help.

SECTION 3: WORKING WITH STUDENTS –
LEARNING ABOUT AND DEALING WITH BULLYING

INTRODUCTION

In order to have an effective anti-bullying policy, the students will need to be involved in helping themselves and one another. Since most bullying happens without adults around, students need strategies they can use when they or their friends are faced with bullying. Also students need to learn to develop empathy and to think about how bullying affects everyone, not just the victims.

This Section has four purposes:

1) To help students learn about bullying

2) To help students learn how to help one another combat bullying

3) To help students practise ways of dealing with bullying

4) To help students develop their own ideas and strategies about how to deal with the bullying problem

You may wish to use some of the exercises in SECTION 1 and SECTION 2 with the students.

3

GETTING STARTED – GROUNDRULES: Lessonplan

Object: To set groundrules for student activities
To encourage students to talk

Time: 40 to 60 minutes

Materials: Large pieces of paper & felt

There are two issues to deal with in this activity:

* the first is to set up Groundrules which will be helpful in all work on bullying done with students.
* the second is to begin to address the feelings the students may have when discussing the emotive problem of bullying.

It is important that the issue of Groundrules is sorted out first to ensure that the students feel comfortable and safe when sharing feelings. Depending upon the amount of time available, you may wish to divide this Lesson into two parts and teach it on different days.

Groundrules

'During this term, we are going to be exploring the problem of bullying.

Some of the things we talk about could be embarrassing or painful or cause you to laugh. The activites will involve some role-playing, writing and discussions with many of the ideas coming from you. So I would like to ask your help to set up some Groundrules. When we have a list of Groundrules, we will discuss them and then agree on which ones we will follow as a class.'

NOTE: If you will be discussing other issues such as personal safety or child abuse, you could also ask the students to brainstorm topics which would be of interest to them. But do not give them the opportunity to do this unless there is a chance to follow through or it will be a pointless exercise.

'We are going to break up into small groups in a moment to brainstorm, but perhaps it would be helpful if I gave you one or two examples of Groundrules.

Let's say we are discussing the problem of bullying and there is someone in the class who is either a bully or a victim. I would like to see a Groundrule which says that we will not name people or make jokes at anyone's expense, and if there is laughter it will not be directed towards someone else.'

3

This might translate into two Groundrules.

Write on the board:

GROUNDRULES

1. Not to embarrass others.
2. Not to make fun of anyone.

Decide how you are going to divide the class (i.e. groups of six, eight, mixed groups of boys and girls, single sex, self-selecting, etc).

'Would you now get into your groups and ask one person to be your scribe or secretary. That person will write the group's ideas on this large piece of paper in big letters.

After you have thought of and written down your ideas for Groundrules, we will put up the sheets of paper so that everyone can see what each group has written. You will have five minutes, so think fast and put down as many ideas as you can during that time.'

Give each group a large piece of paper and a felt-tip marker.

It may be that your students will need longer or shorter time to brainstorm. When the students have completed the Groundrules sheets, bring them together as a large group and have each group put up their ideas.

As the groups share their ideas for Groundrules, write them on the board (or have a student do this) without comment. It usually works better if you take one idea from each group and then go around again. Otherwise, one group may give all the ideas and the other groups will get bored or restless.

When you have recorded the Groundrules, decide which ones are agreeable to everyone. One class listed the following Groundrules:

- Not to embarrass others
- Not to make fun of anyone
- Allow time to talk
- No put-downs
- What is said in the lessons is confidential
- To be supportive of others
- No-one is allowed to talk for more than two minutes at a time
- No-one to act like a wally
- No violence
- Class votes on who to invite in to speak
- Teacher willing to talk privately to students, but not able to promise confidentiality if s/he thinks the student is at risk of serious bullying or some other problem like child abuse.

KIDSCAPE: How to stop bullying

This last Groundrule was suggested by the teacher, who in this case was willing to spend the extra time. You will need to decide that for yourself.

When the Groundrules are agreed, have someone make a poster-type list which is posted up in the classroom.

You may want to agree a plan in case someone breaks the Groundrules. What consequences will follow? One class decided that anyone who broke the rules would be made to write up ideas about the activity and present them to the class. You may decide to exclude someone from an activity, but there is always the possibility that the student is reacting because the issue hits too close to home.

Feelings

The second task is to deal with the feelings which may arise from discussing emotive and embarrassing issues. We suggest that you ask the students to go back into their groups and make another list of possible feelings which may arise while talking about bullying.

Ask that they again appoint a scribe and come up with a list in five minutes.

'We are now going back into the same groups to brainstorm about the types of feelings which may come up when discussing some of these topics. For example, when talking about bullying, some people may feel angry, others may feel scared. So there are many different ways of reacting to these issues.'

Write down some of the possible feelings on the board to give the students a model. Then ask them to go back into their groups and give them five minutes to brainstorm.

Allow more time if the exercise is bringing out productive discussion. When they have finished, again make a list of possible feelings, taking one or two initially from each group. The list might read:

- Angry
- Hurt
- Fearful
- Happy
- Sad
- Disgusted
- Mean
- Furious

It is important to make a collective list so that the students will know that it is alright to have these feelings and that it is normal. It sets the tone for the work to follow.

'There are feelings that many people have when talking about some of these situations. For example, one person might be furious if his or her little brother was beaten up and another might feel happy. It will be important as we discuss all the issues to recognise your feelings and talk with someone about them. You may want to think of who you could talk to, like a gran or mum or dad, a friend, a teacher, etc.'

Here you must again decide if you want to be available for the students for private or small group talks. Students will choose their confidants, but sometimes it is comforting to know that a teacher or youth worker or another adult has made the offer of listening (without making promises of confidentiality in case you have to deal with a serious problem).

The list of feelings is not necessarily for display. The purpose is to bring the idea of expressing feelings into the open. You may wish to continue the discussion by asking the students to think of acceptable ways of expressing feelings. When going through the activities, there will be opportunities to turn feelings into positive steps. For example, if students are angry about bullying, there are ways of coming to grips with the problem by turning the anger into action like setting up bullying arbitration 'courts'.

3

KIDSCAPE: How to stop bullying

AWARENESS-RAISING: *Nine Exercises*

EXERCISE 1 – WHAT IS A BULLY?/WHAT IS A VICTIM?

Divide the class into groups. Ask each group to come up with ten attributes of bullies (aggressive, violent, mean, sneaky, cruel, etc.) After ten minutes, bring the class back together.

Divide the chalkboard or flipchart into two columns. Head one column Bully and the other Victim.

Ask one person from each group to call out in turn one item on their list. Write each group's ideas in the Bully column (only write each trait once – there will be duplication between groups.

Repeat the above Exercise asking for ten attributes of victims (shy, weak, tearful, sensitive). Write these ideas in the Victim column on the board.

In discussion ask:

* Does everyone agree with what is on the board?
* Have any important attributes been left out?
* Are all the attributes on the board negative? (for example 'confident' might have come up in connection with bullies but confidence is not of itself a negative attribute)
* Why are these positive attributes seen as negative when it comes to bullying?

EXERCISE 2 – DISCUSSION TOPICS

● **Telling**

Ask students to discuss when it is right to tell about incidents of bullying:

* Do they think of telling as sneaking, grassing, telling tales, etc?
* Is right to tell if telling will help another person out of trouble or other difficulties like bullying?
* Is it right to tell if telling means getting other people into trouble?
* Is it right to tell to protect yourself?
* When would it be wrong to tell?

● Follow-up Questions

* Is it right to tell what you have seen if you witness someone being robbed in the street?
* Is it right to tell if you see a younger pupil being bullied by someone in your Year?
* Is it right to tell if people you thought were your friends start picking on you and being really mean?
* Is it right to tell if one day you and some friends bullied someone else?
* If you were in a Young Offenders Institute and you were being bullied, would you tell? (The taboo against 'grassing' is very strong amongst offenders)

● Witnessing Bullying

Ask students to think about those involved in bullying incidents:

* What about the bully or bullies
* What about the victim or victims
* What about others who see what is going on but do nothing to stop it?
* Would they just walk past?
* If people do walk past and do nothing, are they to blame?
* Should you get into trouble if you don't help?
* What could they do to help the victim/s?
* If they were in a Young Offenders Institute and they knew someone was being bullied, would they tell?

It is important that students understand that, where bullying is concerned, there is no such thing as an 'innocent bystander'. If someone sees what is going on and does nothing to stop it, or does not tell or get help, then that person is part of the bullying.

● Gangs

Ask students to discuss bully gangs:

* Are those in a bully gang all equally to blame?
* Who is most to blame?
* What could you do if you had become involved in a gang and you wanted to quit but were frightened of the leader?
* What could you do if you knew someone was being bullied by a gang?
* How would you go about breaking the power of the gang?

KIDSCAPE: How to stop bullying

EXERCISE 3 – ROLEPLAY

Ask each group to make-up a roleplay about a bullying incident. (This will probably take a whole lesson).

You can use the roleplays provided later in this Section, if you wish.

Next lesson, ask each group to perform their roleplay.

After each roleplay, ask the other groups for suggestions:

* How conflict could have been avoided?
* Could the victim/s have said or done anything which would have deterred the bully?
* What could witnesses have done?
* What can be done after the incident to help the victim?
* Should the bully(s) be punished or counselled, or both?
* Can anyone give any reasons why the bully behaved in this way?
* What can be done to make sure the bully doesn't behave like this again?

Go through each roleplay again, 'freezing' the action at critical points and incorporating the alternative actions or words suggested by the rest of the class.

Ask the class to consider the following questions:

* Is the outcome different?
* Does the victim manage to avoid the bullying? Is there anything in common between the various alternative strategies suggested?
* Is it possible to draw conclusions about the best way to avoid bullying? (Walk away; say No; ask friends to help; tell an adult; etc).

3

EXERCISE 4 – 'I WAS BULLIED'

Ask pupils who have been bullied to write a short story or poem describing how they felt. If some students have never been bullied, ask them to imagine a victim's feelings.

If anyone has ever bullied anyone else, even a brother or sister, ask them to write about how they felt and why they bullied on that occasion (don't expect a lot of volunteers for the bullying essay!)

EXERCISE 5 – TV, FILMS AND BOOKS

Ask the students to think of bullying situations they have seen in films or TV programmes (even Soaps!) or read about in books.

Ask them to describe briefly what happened:

* Were the scenes scary to see or read about?
* Did they sympathise most with the victim or with the bully?
* Could the victim have reacted differently and prevented the bullying?
* Does bullying only happen in schools?
* Is it easy to identify when bullying is going on?

EXERCISE 6 – HOLD AN ANTI-BULLYING WEEK

Produce a magazine, design posters, show videos like Sticks and Stones, have an assembly with readings of stories and poems written by students, write a play about bullying and perform it to parents or use playscripts.

EXERCISE 7 – PRODUCE AN ANTI-BULLYING MAGAZINE

Pupils from different Years meet once a week (perhaps at lunchtime with a parent volunteer) to discuss what bullying is, make up and act out role-plays; write stories about bullies and victims; make up poems, quizzes, rap songs, puzzles and draw pictures which they make into a magazine. During the Anti-Bullying Week sell the Magazine to everyone connected with the School. (Have an Anti-Bullying page in the School Magazine with problems, poems and puzzles.)

EXERCISE 8 –
HOLD AN ANTI-BULLYING POSTER DESIGN COMPETITION

All students should be encouraged to take part. Display the posters during the Anti-Bullying Week. Use the money raised by selling the Anti-Bullying Magazine to fund prizes for the best poster designs. Convince a local business or local printer to print the best design as the School Anti-Bullying Poster. Display it in every classroom and in the corridors.

EXERCISE 9 – MAKE UP A MULTIPLE CHOICE QUIZ

Get a class or group to make up a Quiz. This exercise stimulates discussion on what is a 'bullying' or aggressive response and what is a 'victim' or passive response. One Quiz Title might be Are you a Bully or a Victim? Each question should be followed by three or four possible answers and each answer should carry a certain number of points.

Example

Have questions like:

1. If someone wants to borrow your calculator when you need it, do you a) give it to them b) say they can have it when you have finished with it c) say no

2. You are on your way home; it's hot and you're really thirsty. You see a younger pupil about to open a can of Coke. Do you a) grab the can b) mutter "I wish I had a Coke" and walk on c) ask if you can have a swig.

Allocate points to each answer (eg. Question 1 a) 1 b) 2 c) 3; Question 2 a) 3 b) 1 c) 2.) Have about 10 – 15 questions. Work it so that the 'Victim' responses have low points and the 'Bully' responses have high points. At the end of the Quiz, provide an 'analysis' of the answers:

eg. If you scored 20 or above, You have bullying tendencies. Careful! You need to think about other people's feelings before you act.

If you scored 10-20, You can be assertive when necessary but you try to consider other people's feelings.

If you scored 1-10, You don't think highly enough of yourself. You tend to give in and put yourself down. Stop Now! Nobody deserves to be a victim.

Distribute the Quiz during the Anti-Bullying Week to other students, or include it in the Magazine.

3

KIDSCAPE: How to stop bullying

CREATING A CONTRACT: *Exercise*

Object: To create a class/tutor group contract

Time: 30 minutes

Everyone puts two or three ideas on a piece of paper. Hold a group discussion with a view to formulating a mutually agreed contract.

Some of the ideas can be fused into straightforward rules for the group which everyone accepts.

Some might be rejected after discussion.
Some might be amended or improved.
Others might spring to mind, having been previously not thought of at all.

This activity will normally be carried out by a class with a tutor, preferably after some introductory discussion about the need for such agreed 'rules'

Areas worth considering for such a contract can include:
the room we work in
the people we work alongside
teachers and adults in charge of us
the school generally
behaviour/attitude around the school
school work, home work
equipment, ours and other people's
newcomers to the school
pupils in need or in distress of some kind
the community in which the school is set.

Try to agree a ten-point contract in the time allowed.

See SECTION 1: SCHOOL CONTRACTS

3

STUDENT MEETINGS: *Notes and Guidelines*

It is important to recognise that a successful and effective anti-bullying policy cannot just be imposed on a group of children/young people. No matter how much staff time and effort has gone into drawing up the policy, it will not be effective unless the students are involved in its creation and implementation. It will be seen by students as just one more set of alien rules imposed upon them by adults. They will not feel that the policy 'belongs' to them and they will have no interest in making it work.

One of the most helpful ways in which children/young people can be involved in the implementation of an anti-bullying policy is through student meetings. These can take various forms:

* Class meetings involving an entire class
* Combined meetings made up of pupils elected from different classes within one year
* Combined meetings made up of pupils elected from the whole student body.

CLASS MEETINGS

The class meeting can be used to discuss a variety of different topics of concern to the pupils and can provide a safe and structured opportunity for pupils to discuss problems openly.

In one primary school the class meeting takes place during the first lesson every Wednesday. The children sit in a circle and the child speaking holds a large, soft ball. (Holding the ball serves to identify the speaker and the other children recognise that they cannot interrupt whilst the speaker holds the ball.) At one meeting, Robin wanted to talk about her pet hamster who had just died; Eliott was worried about a music exam; and Fahim had been pushed around by some older children in the lunch queue. As the meetings took place regularly and their format was familiar, the children felt safe and so were able to talk freely. Some of the other children talked about pets which had died or about music exams they had taken, and the teacher was able to discuss the pushing incident with the class. The children decided that pushing in queues was wrong and the teacher agreed to talk to the older children's teacher about the incident.

Class Meetings can also discuss problems of common concern like bullying within the class and work out solutions acceptable to the whole group.

KIDSCAPE: How to stop bullying

COMBINED MEETINGS

Education for Citizenship was identified as an important cross-curricular theme by the National Curriculum Council and student meetings provide students with practical experience in making collective decisions which have a positive outcome for the whole group. Obviously, as in any democracy, there has to be shared power, so the students' decisions may be subject to review by the Head.

These meetings might consist of eight or ten pupils elected by the student body. A Link Teacher should be appointed to liaise between the elected members and the rest of the staff. This Link Teacher provides support for the members and attends meetings.

Student Meetings can discuss any topic of concern to the students including issues like undertaking a school survey on bullying, how to stop school property being damaged, how to stop littering, supporting new pupils, putting on interesting school assemblies etc. They can make appropriate decisions and give advice and opinions about school policies. The more their ideas are incorporated, the more the students seem to feel the responsibility to become positively involved in the school.

Student Meetings can also discuss ways to stop bullying incidents, teasing and harassment. This means that the children/young people can actually be involved in giving their opinions about what should happen about bullying (see Student Councils/'Bully Courts').

GUIDELINES FOR STUDENT MEETINGS

Student Meetings:

* provide a forum for children to discuss problems and issues
* give shy or quiet children an opportunity to express their feelings
* give children practice in articulating feelings and problems
* help to improve communication skills
* give children practice in listening to others
* give pupils experience of working as a group towards the solution of both individual and group problems
* encourage children to help and support each other
* enhance the cohesiveness of the group

One of the first tasks the newly introduced Student Meetings could tackle might be discussing codes of behaviour or rules to be included in the School Contract. This would give the pupils the chance to discuss what sort of behaviour is acceptable to them and to establish some ground rules for the future.

Teachers may groan at the thought of introducing yet another item into an already top-heavy schedule but the Meetings needn't take long and could fit into a Drama or History period as a class exercise.

STUDENT COUNCILS/'BULLY COURTS': *Notes and Guidelines*

Student Councils have been set up in several schools to deal with incidents of bullying, hence the student title of 'Bully Courts'. The idea was suggested by a young teenager who was fed up with the bullying going on in her school. 4 to 6 children and young people are elected on to the Student Council by their peers and the teachers (see Guidelines in this chapter) to find out what has happened in a particular incident of bullying and to suggest solutions. A teacher or staff member acts as a monitor or link person.

The idea of students being involved in 'bully courts' has caused some controversy. It has been wrongly assumed that they have a purely judicial and punitive role within the school. This is not the case. Their role is much wider and much more positive.

However, Student Councils do provide an accessible and structured forum in which the elected students can discuss specific bullying incidents. The bully could be allowed to choose whether to talk to the Student Council or to the Headteacher. The Council can find out what happened between bully and victim and can then decide what should be done to protect the victim and try to stop the bullying and possibly get help for the bully. This does not imply the imposition of some draconian punishment – School Councils have opted for a time out place for the bully to cool off, suggested ways the bully could be more effective in making friends or have imposed sanctions like eating at a separate table or playing alone for a week.

This system works best with minor bullying incidents. It might not always be appropriate for more serious incidents to be discussed by the Student Council. This is usually the case if the family circumstances of bully or victim have a bearing on the situation, or if issues of confidentiality are involved.

Peer cooperation and pressure is one of the most effective ways of dealing with bullying and the meeting can make it quite clear to all students that bullying in any form will not be tolerated.

Large schools and institutions might have several committees or 'courts' responsible for different years. Using Student Councils to help arbitrate in bullying incidents directly involves students in maintaining the anti-bullying policy and gives them a stake in its success. They are actively involved in enforcing a no-bullying policy which they themselves have helped design. They feel they 'own' the policy. This doesn't meant that adults wash their hands of the policy or its enforcement but it does mean that students can monitor the behaviour of their peers and have the confidence to stop unacceptable behaviour.

3

KIDSCAPE: How to stop bullying

A well-run 'bully court' can teach children a great deal about the responsibilities they have as members of a community.

KIDSCAPE has monitored 'bully courts' in 30 schools and on average bullying has dropped by 30-60% in each of these schools. Indeed in one school the court never had to sit; the mere thought of appearing before it acted as a sufficient deterrent to bullies. However, the 'bully courts' were part of a whole school anti-bullying policy and it was impossible to know how much of the drop in bullying was due to the 'courts' and how much was due to the anti-bullying ethos in the schools. KIDSCAPE has always recommended that 'courts' be part of a whole school plan to eradicate bullying and never used in isolation.

The concept of 'bully courts' has been dramatised in the video Sticks and Stones (see SECTION 3).

3

GUIDELINES FOR STUDENT COUNCILS ('BULLY COURTS')

Setting up the Council

First appoint a member of staff as Link Teacher or Co-ordinator. This person will be responsible for setting up the Council, attending sessions, liaising with the rest of the staff when necessary, and ensuring that decisions taken at the Council are reported back to the students and to the staff.

The Link Teacher may:

* explain to students that a forum will be created to which they can elect members and which will have powers to discuss issues of concern to the whole school and to make appropriate recommendations or decisions (be prepared for initial scepticism: students won't believe the Council is really 'theirs' until they see that the staff are prepared to listen and to let them decide some issues for themselves)

* decide how many members the Council will have – (you may have several Councils depending upon the size of your school, but we suggest 4 to 6 as a workable number)

* ask each class or year to nominate candidates

* draw up a list of candidates

* ensure each class has a copy

* arrange a ballot class by class

* inform student body of the results of the election (the term of office of each elected member will depend on school circumstances but a term is probably about right)

* arrange for the Council's decisions to be relayed to the rest of the student body, if appropriate (announcements in each class the day after the meeting; decisions posted on a noticeboard)

* encourage elected members of the Council to tell their fellow students about the Council's discussions. It is important that information about what goes on at Council circulates as appropriate, otherwise the Council could be seen by students as secretive and untrustworthy

3

* arrange for a Suggestions Box to be placed somewhere prominent and explain to students that they can suggest topics or issues, such as vandalism, littering etc for the Council to address

Basic Rules:

1. Council meetings take place regularly at set times and last for a specific period

2. Everybody listens to the person speaking and nobody interrupts. However, you may wish to agree a time limit or one person could dominate the entire meeting

3. Sarcasm and verbal bullying are outlawed

4. The purpose of the Council is to discuss issues openly, but not to embarrass anyone or to belittle or mock them

Running the Student Council

After the first few Council meetings, everyone will be familiar with the way the Council operates but the Link Teacher may have to provide guidance in the early meetings. The idea is for students to run the whole meeting themselves. How often the Council sits will depend on school circumstances: once a fortnight or once a month would be a good starting point.

* at the first Council meeting, decide a rota from the elected representatives for the chair so that a different person chairs each subsequent meeting (this will need to be done after each election)

* arrange a similar rota for secretary – this person will take minutes at each meeting and record all decisions

Responsibilities as part of whole school anti-bullying policy

The Student Council could be responsible for making recommendation about breaches of the rules listed in the School Contract, including vandalism or bullying, unless the incident was serious enough to involve the police, i.e. assault, or involved a family problem which made open discussion inappropriate.

When discussing a particular bullying incident, the representatives would talk to the victim, the bully and any witnesses to try to find out exactly what happened and why. This would involve:

* asking the parties involved or who have witnessed the incident to write down what happened and give copies to the Council

* inviting the parties individually to come in and have their say about what happened

* calling in additional 'witnesses' if needed

* discussing the situation as a whole Council with the Link Teacher

* coming up with recommendations which are passed on to the Headteacher for action or, if appropriate are given to the parties involved by the Council with the Link Teacher

The decision of the Council regarding the incident would be binding on all parties, but there would be a right of appeal to the Headteacher.

The Council's decision would be written down and a copy given to all parties involved.

If it is not considered appropriate for the whole Council to discuss specific incidents, a sub-committee could be formed to discuss cases of bullying and other student disputes.

Before allowing the students to make recommendations in bullying incidents, parents, governors, the student body and the whole school staff could be invited to see a mock incident being discussed.

It must be emphasised that a Student Council which makes recommendations in bullying incidents will only be successful as part of a whole school policy. *It will not work in isolation.* All the initial groundwork, discussing school contracts and focusing on bullying as unacceptable, has to be done first. It is important that the students realise that there are no innocent bystanders in bullying – if you walk past a person being bullied and do nothing to help then you are culpable. Students have to understand that the responsibility for eradicating bullying is shared by everyone. It is in this context that bullying is an appropriate issue to bring before the Student Council.

Once students realise that they are able to take important decisions themselves, they become very enthusiastic about Student Councils. However, the system will only work if the staff are also hundred-percent committed to the success of the Council.

The benefits can be great as the Council:

* gives students practical experience of democratic process

* gives students an opportunity to discuss issues and problems of concern to them

3

* develops communication skills

* fosters school unity

* encourages students to find practical solutions to common problems

* gives students a stake in ensuring the success of the school's anti-bullying policy

* makes it clear to students that bullying is something they can help solve

* can reduce time taken by staff to sort out student problems

* encourages elected students to accept responsibility

* encourages group initiative

* can be used to encourage student projects like fundraising or organising special events

* teaches students that the school, its policies, problems and successes belong to them as much as to the staff and governors.

Student Meetings and Student Councils are not mutually exclusive and can be used together.

Many schools do not feel that Student Councils are appropriate and that the teachers and governors should be dealing with issues such as bullying. If this is the case, perhaps the Councils could be constituted to discuss issues or a Council set up as a 'bully court' could dramatise the problems of bullying.

Further Reading and other Resources:

Joan Brier/Yvette Ahmad: Developing a School Court as a Means of Addressing Bullying in Schools, in Practical Approaches to Bullying, ed. Peter Smith and David Thompson, David Fulton Publishers , 1991.

Michele Elliott: Bully 'Courts' in Bullying, A Practical Guide to Coping for Schools, ed. Michele Elliott, Longman, 1991.

School Councils (UK)
c/o Priority Area Development (PAD)
3 Childwall Bank Road
Liverpool, L16 7PH
Tel. 0151 722 6822

PAD has been running Pupil Councils in Liverpool schools since 1991 and has a brochure available with details of how to introduce and run these Councils called: 'Growing up with Pupil Councils: An Information Pack'. This is available from PAD at the above address.

USING ROLEPLAYS: *Exercises*

Object: To help children and young people develop and practise effective ways of dealing with bullying

Time: 15 minutes

Materials: Copies of roleplays below or roleplays made up by the students

PRIMARY SCHOOL ROLEPLAYS

These roleplays are extracted from the KIDSCAPE Primary Child Protection Programme. They are part of a lesson on bullying and are included here as an example.

BULLYING

This roleplay can be done by two children or by teachers acting the parts of children. It shows a child being bullied and feeling as if she can do nothing to help herself. There should be some discussion between this and the second roleplay about how to cope with bullies and what the bully and victims might be feeling. For more details, consult the KIDSCAPE Primary Programme.

Ask the children: "How many of you have ever known a bully?"
"Can anyone tell me what a bully is and what bullies do?"

"Now we are going to act out a little play. It's about a child called Alice. (If there is a child in the class called Alice, remember to change the name!) The play starts with a girl called Lucy throwing a ball against the wall in the school playground. While you are watching, think about what you would do if this happened to you."

PRIMARY ROLEPLAY 1 – THE PLAYGROUND BULLY

This Roleplay needs two characters:

(LUCY IS PLAYING WITH A TENNIS BALL: THROWING IT AGAINST A WALL AND CATCHING IT. ALICE IS WATCHING HER FROM A DISTANCE)

LUCY One...two...three...four...
ALICE Hi Lucy give us a catch then
LUCY Hold on a minute, I'm in the middle of something. Eight...nine...

ALICE	(SNATCHING THE BALL OUT OF LUCY'S HANDS AS SHE IS ABOUT TO CATCH THE BALL)Look at that! Brilliant! What a catch!
LUCY	Oi! Hold on...
ALICE	I said give us a catch didn't I?
LUCY	I was going to..
ALICE	Well, that's all right then innit? Come on then, catch this! (SHE THROWS THE BALL QUITE HARD AT LUCY)
LUCY	(DROPPING THE BALL) Hey, not so hard!
ALICE	Stop whingeing and throw me the ball
LUCY	I don't want to play anymore
ALICE	(STERNLY) Throw me the ball, Lucy!
LUCY	I've got to go home. Honest
ALICE	Too bad. We're playing catch. Throw me the ball
LUCY	Oh come on Alice, please. I've got to go (ALICE GOES TO LUCY AND SNATCHES THE BALL OUT OF HER HANDS)
ALICE	Look, Lucy, don't mess me around, all right? (SHE THROWS LUCY THE BALL SOFTER THAN BEFORE. LUCY CATCHES IT)
ALICE	O.K now give me a catch (RELUCTANTLY LUCY THROWS ALICE THE BALL)
END	

Dicuss what Lucy could have done differently and how she is feeling. Why do the children think that Alice is a bully?

PRIMARY ROLEPLAY 2

This roleplay needs three characters.

"Now we are going to act out the second part of this little play. Let's see what Lucy does on the next day. This time, Lucy is playing with a friend called Claire." (If you use the stories instead of the roleplays, stop the story at an appropriate point so that the children can practise shouting 'no' again)

ROLEPLAY 2 – THE PLAYGROUND BULLY

(LUCY IS PLAYING CATCH WITH HER FRIEND CLAIRE)

LUCY	It was horrible! she just wouldn't let me go. I was really late. My mum was livid and I couldn't tell her why – I didn't dare. She said she was going to come back today too. I hate her! (THEY CARRY ON THROWING THE BALL TO EACH OTHER)
LUCY	Twenty eight...twenty nine...Listen Claire. If she comes up today, don't leave me, right?

CLAIRE	All right
LUCY	We'll just keep on playing, yeah. Maybe she'll go away if there's two of us. We could just tell her we don't want to play with her
CLAIRE	OK maybe she won't come anyway. Thirty one...thirty two...(ALICE APPEARS AT A DISTANCE)
ALICE	Oi! Lucy! Give us a catch then! You clear off, Claire! Come on, Lucy! Let's see how far you can throw the ball!
LUCY	(TO CLAIRE) You stick around, right! You promised, remember
CLAIRE	Sure
ALICE	Come on don't mess me about. Throw me the ball!
LUCY	No I won't Alice. Just leave us alone. I'm playing with Claire
ALICE	Not anymore you're not. You're playing with me! Bye-bye, Claire
LUCY & CLAIRE	**NO! You clear off. Leave us alone. We don't want to play with you!**
ALICE	Well you don't huh! Well, too-
LUCY	No we don't. And if you don't leave us alone, I'll tell my mum. And I'll tell her why I was so late home the other day too
CLAIRE	Yeah, and I'll tell my big brother
ALICE	Oh shut up. Both of you! I don't want to play your rotten game anyway. Ya pair of big babies (ALICE LEAVES: CLAIRE AND LUCY LAUGH AND CARRY ON PLAYING)
END	

POINTS TO STRESS:

* Tell someone
* Ask a friend to help you
* You can say "NO"

SECONDARY ROLEPLAY 1

This roleplay is taken from Teenscape by Michele Elliott. It can be used with four or more people. The members of the bully gang can be increased from two to four, making the total six. If it gets much larger, it might be difficult to control.

The characters are: Philip and Linda (victims), John or Liz (leader of bullies), Tony, Chris, Pat, Jamie (members of bully gang)

Philip and Linda are waiting at a bus stop. They talk quietly to each other and scan the distance for the bus. After a minute, a group of young people appear, walking towards them. As they pull closer to the kids at the bus stop, John makes a comment.

3

John:	'Hello, hello...what have we here?' *(other gang members come over to Philip and Linda)*
Tony:	'Aren't they sweet?'
Chris:	'Regular young lovers, I'll bet!'
Linda:	'Get lost, creeps!'
Pat:	'Oh listen to her. Brave ain't ya?'

(The gang surrounds Philip and Linda, and begins flicking at them, but not touching them. Philip raises his fists.)

Philip: 'Leave off, you jerks!'

Gang laughs and comments:

'Couple of wallies'
'Guess they want a fight'
'Can you believe the trash around here?'

Then Linda pushes Chris really hard and Philip hits Tony. A general fight ensues which leaves Linda and Philip on the ground. The gang grabs their watches, empty their pockets of money and then runs off laughing.

Questions to class:

* What would you do if a situation like this happened?
* If the gang was caught, what should happen to them?
* Could Linda and Philip do anything differently?

SECONDARY ROLEPLAY 2

Same scenario as the first roleplay.

John: 'Hello, hello...what have we here?'

(Other gang members join in as before)

Philip and Linda completely ignore them and begin to walk away.

(Gang follows, trying to get the pair to fight, insulting them, but not hitting)

Philip and Linda continue walking, talk to each other and head towards a shop.

(Gang continues to follow them, but are getting bored)

Philip and Linda walk into the shop and the gang wanders off, trying to act big.

Questions to class:

* What else could Philip and Linda have done?
* Should they report this? To whom?
* What if gang is waiting for them when they leave?
* What if the gang had physically attacked them?

Follow-up

Make your own roleplay about bullying

3

WHAT IFS?: *Exercise*

What If? questions can help you think about what to do in case anything should happen. There are no right answers because every case is different. Use the question with your parents or with friends and decide what you think might work? Think of your own solutions and make up new What If? questions to answer.

1. You are walking to school and a gang of older bullies demands your money, skateboard, trainers, etc? Do you:

   a. Fight them?

   b. Shout and run away?

   c. Give them the money?

   * Give them the money (or other possessions) – your safety is more important than money.

2. You are on the school playground and someone accidently trips you? Do you:

   a. Hit the person hard?

   b. Give him or her a chance to apologise?

   c. Sit down and cry?

   * Give the person a chance. If it was an accident, then he or she should say sorry.

3. You are in the school toilet and an older student comes in, punches you and then tells you not to do anything or 'you'll get worse'. You know who the person is and you have never done anything to him/her. Do you:

   a. Wait until the person leaves and then tell a teacher?

   b. Get in a fight with him/her?

   c. Accept what happened and don't tell?

   * You didn't deserved to be punched and the bully was wrong to do it. If you don't tell, the bully will just keep on beating up other kids.

4. You are walking in the lunch room and someone yells out a negative comment directed at you. Do you:

   a. Ignore it?

   b. Yell back?

   c. Tell?

   * You can either ignore it (if it is the first time and that's all that happened) or tell if it really bothers you.

5. A gang of bullies gets you alone and starts beating you. Do you:

   a. Do nothing – just take it?

   b. Fight back?

   c. Shout to attract attention?

   d. Watch for your chance and run away?

   * You must decide, but Answers c & d together would work very well. It would be quite difficult to fight a whole gang of bullies and you might be badly hurt if you did.

6. Someone in your class makes rude comments about you and says them loud enough for you (and others) to hear. It really upsets you. Do you?

   a. Ignore the comments?

   b. Confront the bully and tell him/her off?

   c. Tell the teacher?

   d. Punch the bully in the nose?

   * You may feel like punching the bully in the nose but you'll probably get into trouble if you do. Try answer a first – ignoring comments is difficult, but can work if the bully gets tired of trying to get you to be angry or cry or show some reaction. Your teacher should be told about the comments to others. If you are feeling brave, tell the bully off. Try practising in the mirror to get the right effect!

7. You see someone being bullied. Do you:

    a. Ignore it, walk by and be thankful it isn't you?

    b. Stop the bully?

    c. Get help?

    ★ Ignoring the bully is cowardly and unfair to the victim. You can try to stop it, if you can do so without getting hurt. Perhaps getting other children to stop it would work. At the very least, yell at the victim that you are getting help and get a teacher or other adult to intervene.

8. Your former 'best' friends start to bully you. This hurts your feelings and you are quite miserable. Do you:

    a. Tell your parents?

    b. Do nothing?

    c. Ring one member of the group and ask why they are doing this?

    d. Try to find a new group?

    ★ Talk to your parents and try to get one or two members of the group to see if you can stop their behaviour. It sometimes works to have the parents, if they are friends, talk to each other. You can also try to find a new group because this group may not be worth having as friends if they are so cruel to you.

9. Your friend's dad recently died and some students are saying and making hurtful comments about it. Do you:

    a. Come to his defence and tell them to stop it?

    b. Ignore it, it will stop eventually?

    c. Let the teacher know?

    ★ Do come to his defence and tell the bullies that their comments aren't funny. Also let the teacher know so that he/she can talk about death and address the fears of the bullying children about their own parents dying. This is why they are making comments in the first place.

3

KIDSCAPE: How to stop bullying

10. A new student comes into your class in the middle of the year and some students are bullying him/her. Do you:

   a. Make an effort to be friendly and invite him/her to eat lunch with you and your friends?

   b. Join in the bullying?

   c. Ignore it – everyone gets bullied at first, so don't join in, but don't help the new student either?

   ∗ Remember how hard it is to be new and do everything you can to make the new student feel welcome by inviting him/her to join in with you. If you see that the new student is being bullied, do tell the teacher.

11. Your friends tell you to skip school or they will bully you. Do you:

   a. Go along with them?

   b. Stay in school?

   c. Get them in trouble by telling on them?

   ∗ They aren't really your friends if they want to get you into trouble and threaten to bully you. Don't go!

12. Someone you know is being bullied because they are fat, (spotty, small, wear glasses, are disabled, have red hair, don't like football, etc.). Do you:

   a. Stand up for them?

   b. Join in?

   c. Let adults know what is happening?

   ∗ They can't help what they are and no one deserves to be bullied because they are different. Stand up for them and tell your parents and the teacher what is happening.

3

KIDSCAPE: How to stop bullying

13. Some students in your school make racist comments to minority groups. Do you:

   a. Ignore it and don't get involved?

   b. Enlist the help of other students and teachers to stop the bullies making these comments?

   c. Hit the kids making comments?

   * Racist comments are wrong and hurtful. Everyone has the right to their own culture and religion. Try Answer b.

14. Someone you know is a bully. Do you:

   a. Try to find out why?

   b. Bully him/her?

   c. Try being a friend and setting a good example?

   * If the bully is someone you can help, try being a friend. The bully may not know how to act properly. Bullies are sometimes quite unhappy and need adult help and counselling to sort out their problem.

15. An adult is bullying you. Do you:

   a. Say nothing?

   b. Tell another adult you trust?

   c. Get some other students together and tell the adult to stop?

   * This is very difficult for children. Best to try to get another adult to help.

16. You see someone being badly beaten on a bus/tube. Do you:

   a. Get off at the next stop?

   b. Help the victim?

   c. Tell the conductor/guard or driver?

   d. Pull the emergency cord?

* If you can help, do so. Also, tell someone in charge. If you can get no help and the person is being badly hurt, pull the emergency cord or button when the train comes into the station.

17. A bully has threatened your little brother. He has begged you not to tell your parents. Do you:

    a. Tell him to handle it?

    b. Confront the bully?

    c. Tell your parents?

    * Your brother cannot handle it or he wouldn't have told you. If you confront the bully, the bully might get a gang together against you. Talk to your brother and see if he'll come home with you to tell your parents because they should know so they can help.

3

DRAW A BULLY: *Exercise*

Object: To get the students to think about how we stereotype bullies and to encourage them to think about the different kinds of bullying – physical, verbal, racial, etc

Time: 20 minutes

Materials: Paper, drawing implements

Ask each child or young person to attempt to draw a bully. They should be told that they are NOT to identify someone they think is a bully, but to draw what kind of person they think is a bully. Take care is using this Exercise so that no one is singled out.

When the children or young people have drawn their bullies, discuss the stereotyping:

Are most of the drawings of boys?

Are girls ever bullies?

Are most of the drawings about physical bullying?

What about verbal bullying?

Do bullies all look like thugs or can they be more subtle? In fact, are some so subtle that the victims are sometimes blamed for the bullying?

Allow time for discussion and encourage points from the students.

3

LABELLED 'HANDICAPPED': *Exercise*

Object: To help students understand what it feels like to be labelled 'handicapped' and to help prevent students bullying children with special needs

Time: 15 minutes

Materials: Copy of the poem below

Ask the students to work in small groups. Ask them to read the poem and discuss it. The author of the poem is unknown, but the source is the Greater London Council, which used to hand the poem out on its own training courses.

No Less A Person

I live in a body labelled: 'handicapped'
Stunted legs and arms askew
I live in a body I wouldn't have chosen
But then few of us do.

People say I'm brave
As though bravery were a choice
I learned early not to scream
For mine is an unheard voice.

The world is competitive
And I'm ill-equipped to compete
But I'm no less of a person
Because I'm not complete.

I live in a body labelled: 'Second Rate'
Though I feel second to none
When Society knows the difference
Then my battle is won.

You can help them to think about the implications with questions such as:

* What does it mean to be brave? Are people with special needs always brave? Tell about a time when you were called brave for something you had to do anyway (such as you were sick or someone died or you were in an accident).

* If you are labelled 'handicapped' or have special needs are you likely to be bullied by others? Why/why not?

3

*   Are people with special needs 'second rate'? Why/why not?

*   How does the person who wrote this poem think others perceive him/her?

*   If you were in a wheelchair or had trouble getting around, would your school be an easy place to negotiate? If not, how could you redesign it to make it easier?

*   How would you make cinemas, public transport and other places or things more accessible to people with special needs?

You may wish to follow this up by asking the students to write their own poems.

3

SPECIAL NEEDS: *Exercise*

Object: To give students an opportunity to discuss some of the difficulties which may face people with special needs and to increase their understanding of other people's needs.

Time: 40 minutes

Materials: Statements for discussion, paper, pens

Ask the students to consider the following statements – or make up your own – on their own and then discuss them in small groups for 5 10 minutes. Ask them to think about if they agree or disagree and why or how people reach these conclusions. Have they heard other people say these things? How do they feel about them? Then ask each group to feed back their conclusions.

Statements:

'Disabled' children cannot attend mainstream school – they should go to special schools.

Eczema is catching.

Asthma sufferers use it as an excuse not to do games or come to school.

Deaf children are slow learners.

Children with special needs that you can't see such as cystic fibrosis should wear a badge so you know they need help.

Children with HIV or parents with HIV should be taught separately.

People in wheelchairs just get in the way.

It is no different if you become 'disabled' or are born that way.

'Disabled' children can't join in games.

You can't talk normally to people who are deaf or blind or who have some other special needs.

3

Questions to provoke further discussion might include:

* If they disagreed with the statements, ask them to explain their reasons.

* Ask the students if they felt they knew enough about 'disabilities' and special needs to decide if the statements were true.

* Would it have helped them decide about the statements if they had more information?

* Ask them how they could find out more about different types of 'disabilities'?

* Ask them how they could find out more about the different special needs people can have?

Follow up Exercise

Ask the students to write a story or a poem imagining that they were in a wheelchair, or couldn't see or hear, or run about. What would be the worst thing and what would be the best thing about such a situation? Would it change them as a person? How?

RACISM: *Exercise*

Object: To examine attitudes, dispel myths and raise awareness of racist prejudices

Time: 40-45 minutes

Materials: Pens, paper, statements for discussion

Ask participants to consider the following statements – or make up your own – for a few minutes on their own and then divide into small groups to discuss them. Ask each group to think about if they agree or disagree with the statements and why. Have they ever heard anyone saying these things? How do they feel about it? Then ask them to feed their conclusions back to the main group.

Statements:

Foreigners are dirty.

All blacks and Irish are stupid.

They don't eat 'proper' food.

Everyone knows you can't trust travellers and gypsies – they are always fighting and stealing.

If we sent them all home we would not have any unemployment.

Indians/Pakistanis own all the corner shops and charge too much.

When they are in this country they should adopt our culture and language and forget their own.

It's always blacks who do the mugging and sell drugs.

Gypsies steal babies.

Black people are lazy.

Why should they have the same rights as us when we were born here?

They take all the best council houses.

Ask the groups to explain the reasons for their conclusions.

Further questions to provoke discussion might include:

* Did any of the students decide who was meant by 'they' in the statements?

* Do the students think they have enough information about various ethnic, religious and cultural minorities to decide what they are like?

* Is it fair to lump people under labels like 'they' and 'all blacks' or 'all Irish'?

* What do the students think about the statements if they substitute other groups, for example, 'All people with red hair are stupid' or, 'Skinny people take all the best council houses'?

3

RIP RIP: *Exercise*

Object: To help students understand how damaging bullying is and how verbal bullying can affect people very deeply

Time: 30 minutes

Materials: Several large cut-out figures of a child – can be done on A3 paper or on lining paper; copy of story below or story of your own

This Exercise can be used to deal with all aspects of bullying, including specific issues such as racist comments.

Ask the children or young people to work in pairs or small groups. Give each pair or group one of the cut-out dolls. Explain that the cut-out figure is a whole, happy person who is going to school one morning feeling good. But comments are made and things done during the day which destroy that whole and happy person. Ask the students to rip their cut-out every time they think the figure is hurt by something in the story you are going to read out:

RIP, RIP: The Thoughts of a Child

I can't wait to get to school. I know it's going to be fun. Oh, look, here come some other kids. I think they go to my school. They're waiting for the school bus.

What are they looking at? Me? They seem to be sniggering and pointing at me. Why are they doing that – I didn't do anything to them.

RIP   RIP

What are they saying? Ugly? They're saying I'm ugly. Why are they saying that – I didn't do anything to them.

RIP   RIP

Here come some other children. Maybe they will stop those kids making fun of me. What are they doing? Oh, they're looking away and pretending not to hear. I wish they wouldn't just stand there and do nothing. I guess they must feel the same way as my tormentors.

RIP   RIP

3

I'll just look at the ground and keep to myself. I'm too ashamed to meet anyone's eyes. Oh, the bus has come, the driver is yelling at me to hurry up. Everyone is laughing.

RIP   RIP

In Maths class I was daydreaming and the teacher drew a red line through my work. The kids giggled.

RIP   RIP

In the playground, the kids from the bus surrounded me and shoved me back and forth. The playground supervisor thought we were all having fun. I wanted to tell her I wasn't. But they told me to shut up or 'you'll get worse'. I didn't tell.

RIP   RIP

At lunch they told no one to sit with me. But.....I never did anything to them – why are they doing this to me?

RIP   RIP

I was washing my hands in the toilet, when they came in. 'Why are you washing your hands? You need to wash your whole body. You stink!' Do I?

RIP   RIP

In science class we studied primates. There were pictures of monkeys. When I left the class, some of them were standing outside and they started making monkey noises and gestures as I walked by. It was the last straw – I screamed at them, tears running down my face 'WHY ARE YOU DOING THIS TO ME – WHAT HAVE I DONE TO YOU?'

RIP   RIP

The teacher heard me screaming. They said I'd been bothering them all day. I got into trouble. I feel like I'm in shreds.

RIP   RIP

RIP   RIP   RIP

At this point the figures will be in shreds. Discuss with the children how it feels to be bullied and what could have happened differently in the story so that the child would not have been destroyed:

* How could the other children at the bus stop have helped?

* How could the bus driver have acted differently?

* If you had been the maths teacher, what would you have done?

* If you had been the playground supervisor, what would you have done?

* If you had seen the child sitting alone at lunch, what would you have done?

* If you had seen what happened in the toilets, how would you have helped?

* If you had been in the hall when the others were tormenting the child, what could you have done?

* What should the teacher who heard the child screaming have done?

Ask the students to compile their ideas into a list called 'How to Help Stop Bullying' and post it up in the class. Remind the students of how comments and actions can affect people and encourage them not to make any RIP statements or actions towards each other and to stop others doing so.

3

'THAT'S MY POTATO!' *Exercise*

Object:
To highlight that the differences between people are more than just "skin" deep.

Time:
45 mins (depending on number of participants)

Materials:
One potato for each person taking part

At the beginning of the Exercise, show everyone your bucket or bowl of potatoes. They all look the same: just like potatoes, in fact.

Then give each person a potato. Ask them to study it for 2 minutes and look for distinguishing features (green marks, 'freckles', shape etc). Once they have looked at it closely, they should give their potato a name and make up a story about the potato:

* what it does in its spare time
* what it likes and dislikes
* how old it is
* whether it likes its relations, and so on

Each person is then given 1 minute (or more if there are only a few participants) to tell their potato's life story.

Once all the stories have been told, all the potatoes are put into a bag or bucket and jumbled up. The potatoes are then spread out on a table and the participants have to come and claim their own particular potato.

At this stage, participants are very keen to find their own potato and they examine the potatoes very carefully, rejecting all those that 'don't look like mine'.

* Ask the students what they have learned during the Exercise?

* Ask students how they think this Exercise applies to bullying?

* Have they learned anything which could help them understand why people might bully those who are different from them?

* How does this Exercise help us to understand that labelling people can be misleading?

It is the small differences that make people individual but they are still all people – all members of the human race. Once you take the time to look at someone and really get to know them, you can see that person is not the same as everyone else. People, like potatoes, are not 'all the same' and differences are no reason to bully anyone – in fact, we should encourage and value differences.

3

The following exercises for students were developed by Eric Jones and Joan Preston, KIDSCAPE Trainers. They can be contacted through KIDSCAPE.

EVER-PRESENT PREJUDICES: *Exercise*

Object: To highlight that perhaps our prejudices are present even when we are trying to suppress them.

Time: Rehearsal time plus 15 minutes or more presentation and discussion

Materials: Posters, little old lady costume

This is a simple 'drama piece' suitable for an Assembly which shows that prejudices and ignorance, do-gooding and putting your foot in it often go together.

Across the front of those viewing come, one at a time, several 'protesters' carrying posters on a stick. One poster says, and the 'protester' carrying it shouts, 'Down with Racism'; another 'Ban Racism'; another 'Down with Fascism'; another 'Ban Communism'; another 'Down with Sexism'; another 'Down with Capitalism', and so on.

There appears a little old lady, clearly aged and bent nearly double, with a simple poster which reads 'Down with Rheumatism!' She is politely pushed out of the way by a strapping young man who delivers the line, 'Come on, old lady, out of the way. You leave this kind of thing to young men'.

There can follow a discussion (or assembly) about disregarding some people's real needs and preferring 'popular issues' or about regarding the contribution made by all sections of society. It can be straightforward – the young man is all out for equality but regards himself as more fit and entitled to shout about it than a real sufferer!

This activity is for young people led by adults, or indeed any group which would find it a useful spring-board for discussion.

EVER-PRESENT PREJUDICES (ASSEMBLY SKETCH)

EVERYONE IS VALUABLE: *Exercise*

Object: To enable members of a group to hear something of their value to the group

Time: Depends upon number in group – about 15 minutes

Materials: Piece of paper per person

This should be a very rewarding activity. It should also be sensitively set up and done by someone who knows the group well enough to lay down a few rules. Every person has a piece of paper which will be folded and passed on as if in a game of consequences. In a circle each member adds a good comment to each paper as it reaches them, until they get back the one they started with. Each person starts by putting their own name at the top. The papers are then passed on and at each subsequent person a brief comment is added highlighting the value of the person whose name is at the top. In due course everyone gets back their own named piece of paper with – hopefully – compliments on it.

At very least we should be able to say that everyone has a place in our group. Ideally every person may have made some contribution to the group, perhaps a task well done recently, good attendance, helpful towards others, a good sense of humour, being a good representative for the group, keeping the room tidy, bringing in posters for the classroom and so on.

It ought to be good for everyone to

* a) think of something good to say about others
* b) read something good about themselves.

Needless to say there is no deliberate attempt to know who said what about whom, but in a compassionate group that is no bad thing either.

EVERYONE IS VALUABLE (GROUP EXERCISE)

3

BALLOON DEBATE – THE VALUE OF US ALL: *Exercise*

Object: To have a brief debate on the different values of individuals

Time: 15 to 30 minutes

This simple and popular game is known as a Balloon Debate. Several people adopt the character of someone they know a little about (somebody from History or from current world figures, sport, entertainment, their religion) and the remainder of the group act as audience. There follows a brief debate set up by whoever is in the chair. These people are in a hot-air balloon and one of them must be jettisoned overboard in order that the others might survive, as the balloon is losing height and might crash! They each make a case for themselves to be saved, citing their value to society, contribution to history or whatever. They do not rubbish other travellers but simply make their own case. When each has stated their case, the audience may be asked to vote, with the person generating the least votes being asked to jump overboard!

For our purpose it may be that we can draw the conclusion that everyone is valuable in their own way.

OR, better still, the Exercise might continue with a simple discussion where everyone is asked to cite the value of and contribution to the group made by someone else. The hope is that everyone will hear something of their own value from another contributor.

This Exercise works especially well with younger children.

3

BALLOON DEBATE – THE VALUE OF US ALL
© Eric Jones

SEMPER BELLICOSISSIMUS!: *Exercise A*

Object: To create samples of rules and practices for a school which encourages as much bullying as possible

Time: 30 minutes

Let your mind fly! Write down, or talk and share as many ideas as you can about what the school which encourages bullying would be like: rules, practices, traditions, events, the routines and curriculum content.

Think about corridors, supervision, staff room, student behaviour, staff behaviour and attitudes, hierarchy structures, duties, the environment and premises, prize giving, assemblies, notice boards and posters.

See SECTION 1: A SCHOOL DESIGNED FOR BULLIES?

SEMPER BELLICOSISSIMUS!

3

SEMPER BELLICOSISSIMUS!: *Exercise B*

Object: To design a Coat of Arms for a school dedicated to Bullying

Time: 15 minutes

Materials: Paper and pens for drawing

This is a fun Exercise where each person draws what could be a school badge for St. Bully's School for Belligerent Children from Aggressive Families. The motto **'SEMPER BELLICOSISSIMUS'** more or less means 'we will be as warlike as we can'. It could be included in the design.

This Exercise is for youngsters, with guidance, to explore what elements of bullying feature in their thinking.

As a follow-up, have the youngsters design a school coast of arms for *'NON SEMPER BELLICOSISSIMUS'* meaning more or less 'we seek not to be belligerent!'

You could also use computers to generate appropriate designs.

SEMPER BELLICOSISSIMUS!
A COAT OF ARMS FOR BULLY PARADISE

3

NOBODY GETS IN HERE: *Exercise*

Object: To explore the futility of our prejudices

Time: 15 minutes

In this Exercise one person plays the part of a manager or landlord choosing who shall get the job, or be able to rent a flat. It can even be a teacher/prefect choosing someone to be Form Rep. or in a team. It could be a bus conductor surveying the bus queue to decide who can get on and take up the one available space on the bus! The 'victims' (applicants) form a queue.

The 'authority figure' (manager etc.) then decides on extreme (comic) reasons for NOBODY being chosen. He may do it alone or with a small group of the class (Management Committee!).

This is a GAME highlighting how stupid various prejudices are and is not intended to embarrass individuals in the group.

FOR EXAMPLE: This activity may go like this ....

I'm sorry, sir, you cannot get on this bus. This is a woman's bus stop.

No, sorry, you cannot have a seat. We don't allow people with glasses on at this stop.

Sorry, miss, if you've got red trainers on you will have to wait.

NOBODY GETS IN HERE (ASSEMBLY SKETCH OR GAME)

3

THE PLANET ZIRCON: *Exercise*

Object: To explore the futility of some bullying and unkind behaviour

Time: 15 minutes

Materials: None – unless you wish to dress up as the visitor from Zircon.

This a fun Exercise where one person plays the part of a visitor from the planet Zircon! The task of the others (or some of the others if some act as audience) is to explain how we treat people with 'deformities' – or how we treat people with different colour skin – or those who are weak or small – or those people we think are too fat, too skinny, too tall, too short or just different to us in some way.

The visitor listens and cross-examines.

Use with children with guidance to explore prejudices and attitudes.

FOR EXAMPLE: This activity may go either way:

The earth people may go to great lengths to explain that we treat everybody equally, in which case the Zircon visitor might cross-examine and ask 'Why?' That requires some explaining and helps to focus people's ideas on equality.

Alternatively the earth people may explain that some people are treated badly or are abused in which case the Zircon visitor still asks 'Why?' which, yet again, leads to thinking through our prejudices and behaviour.

THE PLANET ZIRCON (ASSEMBLY SKETCH OR GAME.)

WHO CAN I TURN TO?: *Exercise*

Object: To discuss and demonstrate how to get help

Time: 15 minutes

Materials: Paper for each student and pen or pencil

Start a spider-graph with SELF in the middle and ask members of the group to add as many 'legs' as possible with a label for each leg, naming persons or groups to whom we can turn for help/guidance.

We ought to be able to discuss and perhaps differ about how these groups help us in different ways and for different purposes, e.g. parents, teachers, youth leaders, peers, The Citizens' Advice Bureau, ChildLine, Samaritans, Helplines, doctors, priests, rabbis, mullahs or other religious leaders.

It may be that we can learn to be more understanding of the idea that we often need help, and that others with more experience can be listened to and indeed ought to be.

WHO CAN I TURN TO?

3

WHO INFLUENCES ME?: *Exercise*

Object: To discuss and demonstrate who influences us

Time: 15 minutes

Materials: Paper and pencil

Start a spider-graph with SELF in the middle and ask members of the group to add as many 'legs' as possible with a label for each leg, naming persons or groups who influences us.

We ought to be able to discuss and perhaps differ about how these groups influence us in different ways and for different purposes (e.g parents, teachers, youth leaders, peers, pop industry, heroes government, the law, advertising industry and so on.)

It may be that we can learn to be more understanding of how we make up our minds – how much we take notice of influences – as well as how much we need to take note of those in authority or those we trust.

WHO INFLUENCES ME?

3

BELONGING: *Assembly Sketch*

Object: To draw attention to people's right to be individuals and to the duty we have to tolerate, work along side and benefit from people's individuality

Time: Rehearsal time plus 15 minutes to put on the sketch

Materials: A few simple hats, shoes and one pair of trainers, some apples and a banana, some umbrellas and a rain coat – note colours and kinds from the script! Copies of the script below

This sketch is meant to be the introduction to a discussion, conducted by a teacher,

OR

as an Assembly, wrapped up in whichever format suits the presenter or the school. It takes the form of a sketch which needs acting out.

'BELONGING!' (ASSEMBLY SKETCH)
© Eric Jones (note: author unknown)

3

Belonging

A Sketch for Six Characters

1 We are here to tell you
2 How very important it is
3 That everybody, and I mean everybody
4 Should really get on well
5 With everyone else.
6 What is needed throughout the whole world
1 Is a little understanding
2 Patience
3 Tolerance
4 Kindness.
5 We are very good friends
6 And we shall get on very well together.
1 One reason of course is that we all wear hats.
 You can see my lovely blue hat. *(Puts it on)*
2 And mine. *(Puts it on)*
3 And mine. *(Puts it on)*
4 Yes I've got a blue hat. *(Puts it on)*
5 And so have I. *(Puts it on)*
6 I've got a red hat.
1 What did you say, a red hat?
2 I couldn't have anything to do with people who wear red hats.
3 Nor could I
4 It's utterly irresponsible to wear a red hat.
5 You must change your hat immediately.
1 Change it now or we can have nothing else to do with you.
6 But there aren't any other hats, and anyway, I like my red one.
1 Then you can't stay here with us.
6 But I thought we were friends.
1 There's no buts about it .....Go!
2,3,4,5 *(In quick sequence)* ... Go! go! go! go!
 Six goes

1 We'd better start again. We are here to tell you
2 How very important it is
3 That everybody, and I mean everybody
4 Should get on really well
5 With everybody else.
1 Just a little understanding
2 Patience
3 Tolerance
4 Kindness.
5 We are very good friends
1 One reason of course is that we all wear shoes.
   You can see my smart shoes
2 And mine
3 And mine
4 Yes I've got smart shoes
5 Yes and I've got these smart trainers?
1 What did you say, trainers?
2 I couldn't have anything to do with people who wear trainers.
3 Nor could I.
4 It's utterly irresponsible to wear trainers.
1 You must change into your proper shoes straight away.
5 But I like trainers. Why should I change?
1 You change your shoes or else...
5 I haven't got any other shoes here.
1 Then you can't stay with us.
5 But that's stupid!
1 Stupid? Get out!
2,3,4 *(In quick sequence)* ...Go! go! go!
   Five goes

3

1 We'd better start again. We are here to tell you
2 How very important it is
3 That everybody, and I mean everybody
4 Should get on really well with everybody else.
1 Just a little understanding
2 Patience
3 Tolerance
4 Kindness.
1 One reason that we get on well is that we all eat fruit.
   Look at my lovely apple.
2 And mine
3 And mine
4 I've got a super banana.
1 You've got what?
4 A banana
1 I can't have anything to do with people who eat bananas.
2 Nor can I.
3 It's utterly irresponsible to eat bananas.
4 But I like bananas.
1 Then you must like them somewhere else.
   Go!
2,3 Go! go!
   Four goes

1   We'd better start again. We are here to tell you

2   How very important it is

3   That everybody, and I mean everybody,
    should get on really well with everybody else.

1   Just a little understanding

2   Patience

3   Tolerance

1   We are always careful to be prepared in case it should rain.
    You see my umbrella.

2   And mine

3   And I have a rain coat.

1   Where's your umbrella?

3   I haven't got an umbrella.

2   Haven't got an umbrella?

1   But we are umbrella people. You must get yourself an umbrella.

3   There isn't an umbrella to be had.

1   If you haven't got an umbrella we can't have you here you must go.

2   Go!

Three goes

3

1   Well we must start again. We are here to tell you
2   How very important it is
1   That everybody and I mean everybody
2   Should get on really well
1   With everybody else.
2   What is needed throughout the whole world
1   Is a little understanding
2   Patience
1   Tolerance
2   Kindness. Take a lesson from us.
1   You will note we are always polite
    Should I meet you in the street I will say,
    Good Morning or Good Afternoon.
2   And I'll say, Hi there!
1   You'll say what?
2   Hi there!
1   You must be joking.
2   No, I just like to say, Hi there!
1   And you mean to continue?
2   Of course.

> *There is a short pause.*
> *One looks hard at two and points to the next exit.*
> *Two goes.*

1   I don't know what the world is coming to. I am here to tell you that
    what matters is to keep yourself to your own kind. Maintain
    traditional behaviour. Refuse to allow any deviations. Have nothing
    to do with the people you suspect are – in fact, when I look at you,
    I'm not at all sure...

*Has been backing away, and finds self in a circle of others who have
returned. They put their heads together in conference and then turn to
face the audience*

3

1   It seems that we should start again.
     We are here to tell you
2   How very important it is
3   That everybody, and we mean everybody
4   Should get on really well
5   With everybody else.
6   What is needed throughout the whole world
1   Is a little understanding
2   Patience
3   Tolerance
4   Kindness
5   Love.
6   We've only got one world
1   Made by one God, Father of us all.
2   We've made rather a mess of things so far folks
3   But we're going to try a little harder.
4   *(to three)* Would you like a banana?
3   Thank you very much *(They start going off together)*
2   *(Going across five and six)* I rather like that red hat, don't you?
5   Yes, I must try one *(They start going off together)*
2   *(looking back at one)* Are you coming with us?
1   Yes, certainly. *(To audience)* Well, that's it.
     Good day to you. *(A little hesitantly)*
     Hi there! *(Leaves stage)*

3

STICKS AND STONES VIDEO: *Exercise for students*

Object: To help young people understand why people bully and to explain the 'bully court'

Time: 60 minutes

Materials: Sticks and Stones video (available from KIDSCAPE and from Central Television)

The Sticks and Stones video was produced by Central Television in consultation with KIDSCAPE. Although designed for secondary students, the video has also been used very successfully with younger students.

Show the students the video and discuss their reactions.

Discussion Points:

1. In the bullying incident in the toilets at the beginning of the video, what should the boy who was bullied do? What would they have done had they witnessed this attack? How do they think the boy is feeling about what happened to him?

2. How would they deal with the boys who took the victim's money and shoved him around?

3. How would they ensure that this sort of thing did not happen in the toilets/bike shed or other areas in the school/institution?

4. Ask them to think about the boy who bullied the young boy on the school bus and is talking to camera about what he did. How do they think the victim felt? If that had happened to them, what would they have done?

5. Do they have any sympathy for the bully?
   Is he likeable? Is he a 'typical' bully?

6. Have any of them ever bullied someone for a bit of fun or because they were bored? Are some kinds of bullying worse than other?

7. There were other students on the bus when the victim was being bullied. What could they or should they have done?

8. Was the victim right to tell? What else could he have done? How could this type of bullying be stopped or dealt with?

9. When Simon went to get help for Kathleen, how do you imagine the staff reacted? How would you respond if you were the member of staff approached by Simon. How do you think that the staff in your school would react?

10. If you were Kathleen, how would you like to see the bullies dealt with?

11. Do you think that the bully, Ramon, bullied other students, as well? What kind of a person do you think she is? Why do you think she is that way? Do you know students like that (NO NAMES, PLEASE) and how do you think they can be helped not to bully?

12. What about Ramon's fellow bullies – do you think they can change their behaviour? How?

13. If you were running the 'bully court', what would you do differently, if anything? Do you think a 'bully court' is a good idea? Could it work in your school? Why or why not?

14. What do you think that Ramon's parents will do when they are notified about Ramon's behaviour?

15. Do you think that peer pressure will make a difference to the bullying in this situation? What do you think Ramon will do now? What do you think Kathleen will do now?

Activities about the Video:

1. Write your own ending to the video, with you 'in charge' of the 'bully court':

   * What questions would you ask?

   * What recommendations would you make?

   * What would you say to Ramon?

   * What would you say to Kathleen?

2. Make up your own 'bully court' scene using a different bullying situation.

3. Break into small groups and ask each group to come up with their own solutions to the Ramon bullying incident. Write them on the board.

4. Write a journal from Kathleen's viewpoint.

3

5. Write a journal from Ramon's viewpoint.

6. Write a poem about the situation described in the video.

7. Draw a picture or mural about what happens two weeks after the 'bully court' has met. Are Kathleen and Ramon friendly with each other? Is the situation worse or better?

8. Make a list of questions you would like to ask Ramon and/or other bullies.

9. Make a list of questions you would like to ask Kathleen and her friends.

10. In small groups, recreate the bully scene between Kathleen and Ramon, but change it so that Ramon is stopped from bullying Kathleen by the other students. What would they say? How could they defuse the situation without becoming physically violent? Ask each group to roleplay their scene for the class.

General Activities:

1. Make up a television advertisement against bullying – make one for primary students and one for secondary students convincing them that bullying is wrong.

2. Make a list of 10 ways to stop bullying.

3. Make up a 'Stop Bullying!' magazine for students your age – include stories, poems, pictures, cartoons, advice page etc. Several schools have used this idea with great success.

4. Have a poster contest.

5. Run a 'bully court' as a drama exercise – use it for an assembly.

6. Think of 10 ways to become a more friendly school or 10 ways to make a friend. Compile a list of the best ideas.

7. Does bullying just happen at school? Discuss the problem of bullying outside the classroom and see if you can come up with ideas to stop this kind of bullying?

8. Make your own drama about bullying – write the script, rehearse and present it to the class. You may wish to stop the action of the play before the end and ask the audience what they think will or should happen.

9. Compile of list of helpful books and organisations dealing with bullying. Make sure everyone gets a copy.

10. If you were in charge of your school, institution or the world, how would you stop the problem of bullying in a kind way?

3

SECTION 4: RESOURCES –
BOOKLISTS AND ORGANISATIONS

INTRODUCTION

It is difficult to keep up with all the resources and organisations available which deal with bullying. We have tried to compile a useful list of both. For a more extensive bibliography, see the excellent Bullying: An Annotated Bibliography of Literature and Resources by Alison Skinner (listed in this SECTION under BOOKS FOR PROFESSIONALS).

If you have suggestions which you think should be included in future editions, we should be grateful if you would contact us.

4

KIDSCAPE FREE BOOKLETS

Send a large, stamped addressed envelope to KIDSCAPE, 152 Buckingham Palace Road, London, SW1W 9TR to obtain a free copy of each of the following booklets. Large quantities of these booklets are also available. Please contact KIDSCAPE for prices.

For Everyone:

Stop Bullying! 20 page booket, illustrated, with suggestions for parents, teachers and children.

For Parents:

Preventing Bullying: A Parent's Guide. 20 page booklet booklet with practical advice for parents.

For Teenagers:

You Can Beat Bullying! A Guide for Young People. 20 page booklet.

4

BOOKS FOR PROFESSIONALS

ASSERTION TRAINING: How to be who you really are
Author: S. Rees & R. Graham
Publisher: Routledge
ISBN0-415-01073-X

BULLIES AND VICTIMS IN SCHOOLS
Author: Valerie Besag
Publisher: Open University Press
ISBN 0-335-0954222-9

BULLYING: An Annotated Bibliography of Literature and Resources
Author: Alison Skinner
Publisher: Youth Work Press
ISBN 0-86155-143-5

BULLYING: An International Perspective
Author: Edited by Erling Roland & Elaine Munthe
Publisher: David Fulton Publishers
ISBN 1-85346-115-6

BULLYING: A PRACTICAL GUIDE TO COPING FOR SCHOOLS
Author: Edited by Michele Elliott
Publisher: Pitman (also available from KIDSCAPE)
ISBN 0-273-62692-2

BULLYING: A POSITIVE RESPONSE
Author: D. Tattum & G. Herbert
Publisher: Cardiff, CIHE

BULLYING AT SCHOOL: What we know and what we can do
Author: Dan Olweus
Publisher: Blackwell
ISBN 0-63119241-7

BULLYING: DON'T SUFFER IN SILENCE:
anti-bullying pack for schools
Author: report based on the outcomes of the DFE-Sheffield University anti-bullying project
Publisher: HMSO, 1994
ISBN 0-11-270879-X

CONFLICT MANAGEMENT IN THE CLASSROOM : A Study
Author: Lesley Saunders
Available from Research Services, Tel. 01372 62853
ISBN 0-9510821-3-2

4

COPING WITH BULLYING IN SCHOOLS

Author: Brendan Byrne
Publisher: Cassell
ISBN 0-304-33071-X

DON'T PICK ON ME: How to Handle Bullying

Author: Rosemary Stones
Publisher: Piccadilly Press
ISBN 1-85340-159-5

HELPING CHILDREN COPE WITH BULLYING

Author: Sarah Lawson
Publisher: Sheldon Press
ISBN 0-85969-683-9

A POSITIVE APPROACH TO BULLYING

Author: Eve Brock
Publisher: Longman
ISBN 0-582-21490-4

POSITIVE SCHOOL DISCIPLINE

Author: Margaret Cowin, Liz Freeman, et al.
Publisher: Longman
ISBN 0-582-08713-9

PRACTICAL APPROACHES TO BULLYING

Author: Peter Smith & David Thompson
Publisher: David Fulton Publishers
ISBN 1-85346-159-8

SOME APPROACHES TO BULLYING (School Governor training)

Author: Des Mason
Available from Governors Support Unit, South Glamorgan Council

TEENSCAPE

Author: Michele Elliott
Publisher: Health Education Authority (also available from KIDSCAPE)
ISBN 1-85448-069-3

TURN YOUR SCHOOL ROUND

Author: Jenny Mosley
Publisher: LDA
ISBN 1-85503-174-4

'YOU KNOW THE FAIR RULE'

Author: Bill Rogers
Publisher: Longman
ISBN 0-582-08672-8

4

WE CAN STOP IT
Author: Hilary Claire
Publisher: Islington Safer Cities Project

WE DON'T HAVE BULLIES HERE
Author: Valerie Besag
Publisher: Calouste Gulbenkian Foundation

VIDEOS

BULLYING: FACE IT, STOP IT, HOW
20 mins. with accompanying notes (32 pages)
Produced by Cumbria Education Service with the Alfred Barrow School, Barrow-in-Furness, Cumbria. Tel. 01228 812083

KICKS AND INSULTS
20 mins.
Produced by Educational Media Film & Video Ltd., Harrow, Middx. Tel. 0181 868 1908/1915

ONLY PLAYING MISS
56 mins. (Playscript also available)
Produced by Neti-Neti Theatre Company, London,
Tel. 0171 272 7302

STAMP OUT BULLYING (the 'no blame approach')
With accompanying book
ISBN 1-873942-10-9
Produced by Lame Duck Publishing, 10 South Terrace, Redland, Bristol, BS6 6TG

STICKS AND STONES with teaching notes
20 mins. for 12-16 year olds
Produced by Central Television in association with KIDSCAPE
Available from KIDSCAPE, Tel. 0171 730 3300

WILLOW STREET KIDS ON THE TRAIL
13 mins. for 6-10 year olds.
Produced by Co-op for KIDSCAPE
Available from KIDSCAPE 0171 730 3300

4

KIDSCAPE: How to stop bullying

BOOKS FOR PARENTS

BAD BEHAVIOUR
Author: Dr. John Pearce
Publisher: Thorsons Publishing Group
ISBN 0-7225-1723-8

CHILDREN UNDER STRESS
Author: Sula Wolff
Publisher: Penguin Group
ISBN 0-14-021548-4

COPING WITH BULLYING IN SCHOOLS
Author: Brendan Byrne
Publisher: Cassell
ISBN 0-304-33071-X

COPING WITH TEENAGE DEPRESSION
Author: Kathleen McCoy
Publisher: Mosby Medical Library
ISBN 0-452-25791-3

THE COURAGE TO GRIEVE
Author: Judy Tatelbaum
Publisher: Cedar
ISBN 0-7493-0936-9

DISCIPLINE – A positive guide for parents
Author: Martin Herbert
Publisher: Basil Blackwell
ISBN 0-631-16875-3

FIGHTING, TEASING AND BULLYING
Author: Dr. John Pearce
Publisher: Thorsons Childcare Series
ISBN 0-7225-1722-X

GOOD HABITS, BAD HABITS
Author: Dr John Pearce
Publisher: Thorsons Childcare Series
ISBN 0-7225-2296-7

HELPING CHILDREN COPE WITH BULLYING
Author: Sarah Lawson
Publisher: Sheldon Press
ISBN 0-85969-683-9

4

HELPING CHILDREN COPE WITH GRIEF
Author: Rosemary Wells
Publisher: Sheldon Press
ISBN 0-85969-559-X

HELPING CHILDREN COPE WITH STRESS
Author: Avis Brenner
Publisher: Lexington Books
ISBN 0-669-08995-8

HELPING YOUR SCHOOLCHILD
Author: Carol Baker
Publisher: Longman
ISBN 0-582-05033-2

KEEPING SAFE
Author: Michele Elliott
Publisher: Coronet/Hodder (also available from KIDSCAPE)
ISBN 0-340-62482-5

THE KID'S BOOK OF DIVORCE
Author: Eric Rofes
Publisher: The Lewis Publishing Company
ISBN 0-394-71018-5

PARENT INFORMATION CHECKLIST
Available from ACE (Advisory Centre for Education) 0171 354 8321
ISBN 0-900029-89-7

POSITIVE PARENTING – Raising Children with Self Esteem
Author: Elizabeth Hartley-Brewer
Publisher: Cedar
ISBN 0-7493-1501-6

STEPPARENTING
Author: Jeannette Lofas with Dawn B. Sova
Publisher: Kensington Publishing Corp.
ISBN 0-8217-1683-2

TANTRUMS AND TEMPERS
Author: Dr. John Pearce
Publisher: Thorsons Publishing Group
ISBN 0-7225-1721-1

THROUGH GRIEF
Author: Elizabeth Collick
Publisher: Darlton.Longman & Todd
ISBN 0-232-51682-0

4

WORRIES AND FEARS

Author: Dr. John Pearce
Publisher: Thorsons Publishing Group
ISBN 0-7225-1893-5

YOUR CHILD'S SELF-ESTEEM

Author: Dorothy Corkille Briggs
Publisher: Doubleday & Company
ISBN 0-385-04020-2

YOUR CHILD STARTING SCHOOL

Author: Peter Bainbridge Jones
Publisher: Hill View Primary School (Tel: 01295 272045)
ISBN 0-9521915-0-4

101 WAYS TO DEAL WITH BULLYING: A GUIDE FOR PARENTS

Author: Michele Elliott
Publisher: Hodder (also available from KIDSCAPE)
ISBN 0-340-69519-6

4

KIDSCAPE: How to stop bullying

BOOKS FOR CHILDREN WHO ARE BULLIED

BOOKS FOR YOUNGER CHILDREN:

THE ANTI COLOURING BOOK
Author: Susan Striker/Edward Kimmel
Publisher: Hippo
ISBN 0-590-70011-1   Age 4+

THE BAD TEMPERED LADYBIRD
Author: Eric Carle
Publisher: Picture Puffin
ISBN 0-14-050398-6   Age 3+

BEING BULLIED
Author: Kate Petty and Charlotte Firmin
Publisher: Bracken Books
ISBN 1-85170-955-X   Age 5-8

BILL'S NEW FROCK
Author: Anne Fine
Publisher: Mammoth
ISBN 0-7497-0305-9   Age 7-9

BOY ON A BUS
Author: Dermot McKay
Publisher: Grosvenor Books
ISBN 1-85239-009-3   Age 7-11

THE BULLIES MEET THE WILLOW ST KIDS
Author: Michele Elliott
Publisher: Piccolo (also available from KIDSCAPE)
ISBN 0-330-32800-X   Age 7-11

BULLY
Author: David Hughes
Publisher: Walker Books
ISBN 0-7445-2169-6   Age 3-6

BULLY FOR YOU
Publisher: Child's Play
ISBN 0-85953-365-4   Age 4-7

4

FEELING HAPPY FEELING SAFE
Author: Michele Elliott
Publisher: Hodder & Stoughton (also available from KIDSCAPE)
ISBN 0-340-55386-3   Age 2-6

FEELING LEFT OUT
Author: Kate Petty and Charlotte Firmin
Publisher: Bracken House
ISBN 1-85170-954-1   Age 5-8

I WON'T GO THERE AGAIN
Author: Susan Hill
Publisher: Walker
ISBN 0-7445-2091-6   Age 3+

MAKING FRIENDS
Author: Kate Petty and Charlotte Firmin
Publisher: Bracken Books
ISBN 1-85170-956-8   Age 5-8

PLAYING THE GAME
Author: Kate Petty and Charlotte Firmin
Publisher: Bracken Books
ISBN 1-85170-953-3   Age 5-8

RHYME STEW
Author: Roald Dahl
Publisher: Jonathan Cape
ISBN 0-224-02660-7   Age 6+

ROSIE AND THE PAVEMENT BEARS
Author: Susie Jenkin-Pearce
Publisher: Red Fox
ISBN 0-09-972090-6   Age 4+

SALLY-ANN IN THE SNOW
Author: Petronella Breinburg
Publisher: The Bodley Head
ISBN: 0-370-01809-5   Age 4+

SOMETHING ELSE
Author: Kathryn Cave
Publisher: Viking/Penguin
ISBN 0-670-8489222-1   Age 3-6

4

THE TROUBLE WITH THE TUCKER TWINS
Author: Rose Impey & Maureen Galvani
Publisher: Picture Puffins
ISBN 0-14-054089-X   Age 4-6

THE TWITS
Author: Roald Dahl
Publisher: Puffin
ISBN 0-14-031406-7   Age 6+

BOOKS FOR OLDER CHILDREN AND TEENS:

CAT'S EYE
Author: M. Atwood
Publisher: Virago   Age 10+

CHICKEN
Author: Alan Gibbons
Publisher: Orion Childrens Books
ISBN 1-85881-051-5   Age 8-12

THE CHOCOLATE WAR
Author: Robert Cormier
Publisher: Lions, Tracks
ISBN 0-00671765-9   Age 9+

DON'T PICK ON ME
Author: Rosemary Stones
Publisher: Piccadilly
ISBN 1-85881-053-1   Age 10-teen

THE FISH FLY LOW
Author: Steve May
Publisher: Mammoth
ISBN 0-7497-1410-7   Age 10+

LORD OF THE FLIES
Author: William Golding
Publisher: Faber and Faber   Age 12+

THE TRIAL OF ANNA COTMAN
Author: V. Alcock
Publisher: Mammoth/Octopus   Age 10+

WHOSE SIDE ARE YOU ON
Author: Alan Gibbons
Publisher: Orion Childrens Books
ISBN 1-85881-053-1   Age 8-12

4

KIDSCAPE: How to stop bullying

ORGANISATIONS WHICH CAN HELP

BOOKSELLERS

Mail Order Booksellers with up-to-date catalogues on bullying and disruptive behaviour:

Abbey Books
4 Bank View Road
Derby
DE22 1EL
Tel: 01332 290021

Bookstall Services
86 Abbey Street
Derby
DE22 3SQ
Tel: 01332 368039

ADVICE AND INFORMATION

Anti-Bullying Campaign
185 Tower Bridge Road
London SE1 2UF
Tel: 0171 378 1446

Advisory Centre For Education
1B Aberdeen Studios
22 Highbury Grove
London N5 2EA
Advice Line: Tel. 0171 354 8321

ChildLine
0800 1111

Children's Legal Centre
The University of Essex
Wivenhoe Park
Colchester, Essex CO4 3SQ
Tel: 01206 873820

4

KIDSCAPE: How to stop bullying

Commission for Racial Equality
Elliot House
10/12 Allington Street
London SW1E 5EH
Tel: 0171 828 7022

Education Otherwise
PO Box 7420
London N9 9S2
Tel: 0891 518 303

KIDSCAPE
152 Buckingham Palace Road
London SW1W 9TR
Tel. 0171 730 3300
Fax. 0171 730 7081

Learning Through Landscapes
Third Floor, Southside Offices
The Law Courts
Winchester
Hants. SO23 9DL
Tel: 01962 846258
Information, books and videos on improving playgrounds

Scottish Child Law Centre
Lion Chambers
170 Hope Street
Glasgow G2 2TU
Tel: 0141 226 3737

Youth Access
1a Taylors Yard
67 Alderbrook Road
London SW12 8AD
Tel: 0181 772 9900

For a more complete list of organisations, see Keeping Safe, 101 Ways to Deal with Bullying or Bullying: A Practical Guide to Coping for Schools, all by Michele Elliott and available from KIDSCAPE.

4